The Norse Hamlet

THE NORSE HAMLET

The Revenge of Amleth
Saxo Grammaticus

The Hystorie of Hamblet
François De Belleforest

Translation and Introduction by
Søren Filipski

Hythloday Press

2013

Cover image: *The Play Scene in Hamlet*, Edwin Austin Abbey, c. 1897

Contents

INTRODUCTION

THE EVOLUTION of the legend that gave rise to Shakespeare's *Hamlet* starts with *The History of the Danes* (*Gesta Danorum* or *Historiae Danicae*) by Saxo (b. 1150?), a Danish cleric, who began his *History* at the request of the Archbishop Absalon of Lund in the late twelfth century. The book was completed sometime between Absalon's death in 1201 and the death of his successor Anders in 1222.

Of the *History*'s sixteen chapters, only the last seven are strictly historical, relating factual events of the twelfth century, which Saxo learned from the personal reminiscences of Archbishop Absalon. The first nine chapters are a treasury of Danish folklore, faithfully compiled from ancient poems and sagas without attempt at critical evaluation. Books III and IV of this first, mythological section contain the story of Amlethus, or Amleth, whose father Horvendile, co-governor of Jutland, is murdered by his brother Feng, who usurps Horvendile's position and marries his widow. Amleth feigns madness while plotting his father's revenge.

Saxo may have partly modeled the tale on the story of Junius Brutus, who, according to the Roman historian Livy, pretended insanity while devising Tarquin's expulsion from Rome. Saxo's story, as retold by authors of later centuries, would beget the inspiration for Shakespeare's *Hamlet*.

In 1431, an anonymous editor added the encomium "Grammaticus," meaning "The Lettered," to Saxo's name. The addition was apt, since Saxo wrote in a difficult, ornate Latin style imitating Valerius Maximus's *Facta et dicta memorabilia* (*Memorable deeds and sayings*) of the first century and Martianus Capella's *De Nuptiis Philologiae et Mercurii* (*On the Marriage of Philology and Mercury*) of the fifth. Saxo's borrowings from Maximus and Capella enrich his vocabulary and raise the literary quality of his Latin high above the often elementary Latin of his Medieval contemporaries. Indeed, so literate is Saxo's style that its erudition may have hindered the *History*'s initial circulation. Since few possessed the skill to read Saxo's Latin, the book lapsed into obscurity for three centuries.

A rediscovery of Saxo began in 1514, when a reprinting in Paris introduced the History to a welcoming Renaissance readership. Though Saxo's Latin had been too lettered for the Medievals, the Renaissance humanists, who honored the elevated Latin of Cicero and Virgil but abhorred Medieval Latin's crudity, found in Saxo a vigorously Classical voice from a country and era they had thought devoid of good writing. The discriminating Erasmus of Rotterdam extolled Saxo's style in his *Dialogus Ciceronianus* (*Ciceronian Dialogue*, 1528):

> BULEPHORUS: I want [to turn our discussion] to Denmark, which has given us Saxo Grammaticus, who has compiled a splendid and magnificent history of his own people.
> NOSOPONUS: I approve of his lively and fiery mind, his astonishing range of vocabulary, his frequent maxims, and marvelous variety of figures, so much that I cannot wonder enough how a Dane at that time could have had such a force of eloquence.

The Elizabethans learned the story of Amleth from a French language adaptation by François (Francis) de Belleforest (1530-83), published in Book V of his *Histoires Tragiques* (1570), a seven-volume collection of exotic stories, which consist mainly of translations from the *Novelle* of Italian sensationalist Matteo Bandello (1480-1565), but also included a retelling of Saxo's account of Amleth.

Belleforest was not an extraordinary writer, but he earned swift popularity in France (with Book V of *Histoires Tragiques* going through seven editions before 1600) because he wrote in the French vernacular just as Latin was lapsing into its final decline as an international language. As the Renaissance drew to a close, the humanists' zeal for Classical languages gave way to a growing need to record history in modern tongues. In the same way that Holinshed's *Chronicles* gave England an accessible history in English, Belleforest was among the first to record history in common French.

Belleforest's tale of Amleth is largely faithful to Saxo, but nearly twice as long: first, because Belleforest adds detail and dialogue, particularly in the place where Amleth reproves his mother for infidelity and incest; and second, because he intersperses his narrative with lengthy, usually theological digressions.

Shakespeare's most immediate source for *Hamlet* was probably not Saxo or Belleforest, but a lost Elizabethan play based on Belleforest and written in the 1580s by an unknown author. Scholars dub this play *Ur-Hamlet*. The evidence for *Ur-Hamlet*'s existence deserves attention, because Shakespeare's Hamlet contains major deviations from Saxo and Belleforest, some of which may have originated in the earlier play.

Our principle knowledge of *Ur-Hamlet* comes from three Elizabethan sources. One is an entry in the accounting book, or "diary," of theater manager Phillip Henslowe (d. 1616), which logs the receipt of eight shillings for a performance of Hamlet by the Lord Admiral's Men and the Lord Chamberlain's Men at Newington Butts. This entry, on 9 June 1594, does not refer to Shakespeare's *Hamlet*, which was probably not written until 1601. While some scholars, have argued plausibly that the 1564 production was of an early draft by Shakespeare, the most likely view is that another *Hamlet*, by a different author, predated Shakespeare's; further, Shakespeare would have known this play since he was among the Lord Chamberlain's Men at the time it was performed. That the performance grossed only eight shillings and the play never appears again in Henslowe's diary suggests that it had lost popularity by 1594.

Henslowe's diary tells nothing of *Ur-Hamlet*'s contents, but two other pre-1601 sources are more revealing. The first is an essay by Thomas Nashe (1567-1601) called *To the Gentlemen Students of both Vniversities* (1589), a satirical assault on what Nashe considered the degenerate state of English literature. The essay, which prefaces Robert Greene's (1558-92) novel *Menaphon* (1589), lampoons playwrights who, lacking the education to read Latin, had been modeling their tragedies upon translations of Seneca:

> It is a common practise now a daies amongst a sort of shifting companions, that runnne through euery arte and thriue by none, to leaue the trade of *Nouerint* whereunto they were borne, and busie themselues with the indeuors of Art, that could scarcelie latinize their necke-verse if they should have neede; yet English Seneca read by candle light yeeldes manie good sentences, as *Bloud is a begger*, and so foorth: and if you intreate him faire in a frostie morning, he will affoord you whole *Hamlets*, I should say handfulls of tragical speeches. But ô griefe! *tempus edax rerum*, what's that will last alwa ys? The sea exhaled by droppes will in continuance be drie, and *Seneca*, let bloud line by line and page by page, at length must needes die to our stage: which makes his famisht followers to imitate the Kidde in *Æsop*, who, enamoured with the Foxes new fangles, forsooke all hopes of life to leape into a new occupation; and these men renowncing all possibilities of credit or estimation, to intermeddle with Italian translations: wherein how poorelie they have plod-

ded, (as those that are neither prouenzall men, nor are able
to distinguish of Articles,) let all the indifferent Gentlemen
that have trauailed in that tongue, discerne by their two-
penie pamphlets: and no meruaile though their home-born
mediocritie be such in this matter; for what can be hoped of
those, that thrust *Elisium* into hell, and have not learned so
long as they have liued in the spheares, the just measure of
the Horizon without an hexameter.

Seneca's tragedies were masterworks of over-wrought
rhetoric and blood; their popular Elizabethan imitations,
especially those dealing with revenge, were equally rhe-
torical and even more bloody. Nashe's mention of *Ur-
Hamlet* in a discourse on imitators of Seneca suggests it
was likewise violent; *Ur-Hamlet*'s quantity of "tragical
speeches" is both a Senecan trait and a famously distinc-
tive feature of *Hamlet*.

Nashe also gives a clue about the probable author of
Ur-Hamlet. "The Kidde in *Æsop*" is likely a pun on the
name of playwright Thomas Kyd (1558-1594) whose
Spanish Tragedy (1590?) was a pillar of Seneca-styled revenge tragedy. The proximity between Nashe's mocking
of *Ur-Hamlet* and his mock of Kyd leads scholars to suspect that Kyd wrote *Ur-Hamlet*.

Though this evidence alone is slight, the case for
Kyd's authorship improves on examination of likenesses
between *The Spanish Tragedy* and *Hamlet*, which suggest
that the former influenced the latter. *The Spanish Tragedy* tells of Heironymo, a general who revenges his son's
death. Like Hamlet, Heironymo delays his revenge, feigns
madness, and presents a play to trap the murderers. *The*

Spanish Tragedy also includes an Ophelia-like character, who goes mad and kills herself when her son is murdered, and scenes of dialogue between the ghost of a murdered man and the spirit of Revenge, a possible protoytpe for the ghost scenes in *Hamlet*. Perhaps, when writing *Hamlet*, Shakespeare amalgamated incidents from *Ur-Hamlet* and *The Spanish Tragedy*. If both were by Kyd, the plots may have blended naturally. Or perhaps Kyd himself recycled material from his own *Ur-Hamlet* when writing *The Spanish Tragedy*. Whether Kyd wrote *Ur-Hamlet* is unprovable, but the evidence for his authorship is better than for any other candidate's.

The third Elizabethan reference to *Ur-Hamlet* comes from Thomas Lodge (1558?-1625), the prolific author whose novel *Rosalynde* was the basis of *As You Like It*. In *Wits Miserie, and the Worlds Madnesse: Discovering the Devils Incarnat of this Age* (1596), Lodge mentions a stage ghost calling for Hamlet to revenge. Since no ghost appears in Saxo or Belleforest, the ghost in *Ur-Hamlet* must have been the original from which Shakespeare derived his own ghost. Evidently, *Ur-Hamlet*'s ghost was of frightening, even demonic stature, for Lodge uses its appearance to describe that of Hate-Virtue, an incarnate son of Belzebub:

> The first by Sathan (his grandsire) was called HATE-VIRTUE, or (in words of more circum-stance) Sorrow for another mans good success) who after he had learnt to lie with LUCIAN, to flatter with ARISTIPPUS, & coniure of ZOROASTES, wandred a while in France, Germanie, & Italy,

to learn languages & fashions, & now of late daies is stoln into England to depraue all good deseruing. And though this fiend be begotten of his fathers own blood, yet is he different frô his nature, & were he not sure y^t Iealousie could not make him a cuckold, he had long since published him for a bastard: you shall know him by this, he is a foule lubber, his tongue tipt with lying, his heart stéeled against charity, he walks for the most part in black vnder the colour of grauity, & looks pale as the Visard of ye ghost which cried so miserally at ye Theator like an oister wife, Hamlet, re-uenge: he is full of infamy & slander, insomuch as if he ease not his stomack in detracting somewhat or some man before noontide, he fals into a feuer that holds him while supper time: he is alwaies deuising of Epigrams and scoffes, and grumbles, murmures continually, although nothing crosse him, he neuer laughes but at other mens harmes, briefly in being a tyrant ouer mens fames, he is a very Titius (as Vergil saith) to his owne thoughts.

"Hamlet, revenge" must have been a famous line from *Ur-Hamlet*, since two other writers quote the same words in later years. In Thomas Dekker's (1572-1632) tragedy *Satiromastix or The untrussing of the Humorous Poet* (1601) Captain Tucca, enraged by a series of epigrams written against him by the poet Horace, declares, "[M]y name's Hamlet reuenge." (IV.i.121) A 1620 poem by satirist Samuel Rowlands (1570?-1628?) also quotes the phrase:

Of two euills chuse the least.
A Scriuener (about nine a clocke at night)
Sat close in's shop, and earnestly did write,
The villany abroad suspecting not,

While two obseruing him, thus layd a plot,
Quoth one to t'other, snatch thou off his hat:
The which he did, and ran away with that:
The Scriuener in hast his shop forsakes,
And for to ouertake him vndertakes,
So while he follows him that runs away
The other rascall watching for his pray,
Enters the shop as bold as bold might be,
And takes his cloake and so away goes he.
Scriuener comes backe, bare headed as he went,
Missing his cloake was far worse discontent,
Quoth he what case am I brought in to night,
Of hat and cloake being vncased quite?
I will not cry *Hamlet Reuenge* my greeues,
But I will call *Hang-man Reuenge* on theeues.

Contemporary references to *Ur-Hamlet* cease with Rowlands, leaving scholars to speculate on how far the lost play influenced Shakespeare. Whether *Ur-Hamlet* added such incidents as the duel with Laertes, the immortal revenge theme, or the Yorick scene cannot be perfectly known, but that Hamlet's ghost certainly originated with *Ur-Hamlet* gives precedent to the supposition that many of Shakespeare's innovations on Saxo and Belleforest were first authored by the writer of *Ur-Hamlet*.

This book contains my translation of the portion of Saxo's *History* that tells of Amleth along with the complete text of the 1608 English translation of Belleforest called *The Hystorie of Hamblet*.

-Søren Filipski

THE REVENGE OF AMLETH
BY SAXO GRAMMATICUS

I
THE EXPLOITS OF HORVENDILE

(GESTA DANORUM, BOOK III, CHAPTER 6)

The beginning of Book III tells of Hother, king of Sweden and Denmark, and of his feud with Odin's son, Balder, for the hand of Nanna, daughter of King Gewar. After a series of battles, Hother kills Balder. Vowing revenge for Balder's death, Odin visits a soothsayer who tells him to beget a son by Wrinda, daughter of the king of the Ruthenians. The boy will one day avenge Balder. Odin rapes Wrinda and she gives birth to Boe, who, having grown to manhood, raises an army against Hother and meets him in battle, where the two kill one another. With Hother dead, the Kurlanders, Swedes, and Slavs revolt against Denmark, but Hother's son, Rorik, now king, suppresses the rebellion.

AT THAT TIME, Horvendile and Feng, whose father Gervendile had been governor of the Jutes, were appointed to his position by Rorik for the defense of Jutland. But Horvendile, after his third year of rule, pursued the height of glory by dedicating himself to piracy. Koller, King of Norway, was emulous of his deeds and great fame, and thought, through superior strength in arms, to ennoble himself by obscuring the famous glory of this pirate.

Searching through the strait he sailed, and came upon Horvendile's fleet. In the midst of the open sea lay an island that each of the pirates controlled, bringing their ships up on opposite sides. The pleasant look of the shores was inviting to the two captains. The outward beauty of the place enticed them to look through the vernal interior of the woods, and to wander through the bright glades and veiled forests. There the paths of Koller and Horvendile chanced to bring them together in the open and without witnesses.

Then Horvendile addressed the king first, asking what sort of combat he preferred, and asserted for his own part that the best battle would be the one that used the strengths of the fewest men. For the duel, he said, was the most effective of all forms of combat for claiming the prize of courage, because it relied only on one's own native strength, excluding the help of another's hand.

Then Koller admired the gallant thinking of the young man and said, "Since you have allowed me the choice of battle, I consider it best to use one which, free of tumult, needs only the labor of two. Certainly it smacks of greater daring and leads to a speedier victory. In this we are of one mind; our separate judgments agree. But since the outcome remains in doubt, we each must respect propriety, and not indulge our desires to the point of neglect the final offices. Hate is in our hearts, but let there also be piety, which in the course of time may take the place of sternness. For although differences of mind divide us, we are still reconciled by the laws of nature, by whose partnership we are tied together indeed, however much our rage disjoins our spirits. And so, let us accept as a condition of piety that the victor shall give funeral rites to the vanquished, for everyone accepts that these are the last obligations of humanity. No pious person will avoid them. Let each army put aside its sternness and perform this duty in peace. May spitefulness depart after death, and rivalry be put to sleep in the grave. Though hatred cut us apart in life, let us not make such a spectacle of cruelty as to persecute each other's ashes. It will be a boasting honor to the victor to have given the loser a magnificent funeral. For whoever pays respects to his fallen enemy earns himself the favor of the survivors, and he who pays humane respect to the dead conquers the living by kindness."

"Yet there is another thing, no less grievous, that sometimes happens to the living: the severing of a body part. I do not consider this calamity to need any less redress than the worst of fates. For those who keep their lives in battle often suffer losing a limb, a doom that is usually considered worse than any death, since death razes the memory of all things, while a living man cannot forget the destruction of his own body. This evil should also be dealt with somehow. Let us therefore agree that the injury of one of us shall be recompensed by the other with ten gold talents. For how much more pious it is to pity one's own misfortunes when one has compassion for another's! All men take counsel from nature; who neglects nature is his own murderer."

When they had spoken and sworn to these things, they fell to battle. They paid no heed to the strangeness of their meeting or the pleasantness of the springtime place, which might have lessened the wrath of their encounter. But Horvendile, his spirit burning too hotly, was more zealous of attacking his enemy than of defending his own body, and had thrown away his shield to hold his sword with both hands. And his bravery did not fail; he stripped

Koller of his shield with a thicket of blows and, hacking off his foot, took his life at last. Then, according to the agreement, Horvendile gave him a royal funeral decked in pomp. Then he pursued and killed his sister, Sela, a seasoned pirate and a master of war.

After spending three years in gallant deeds of battle, he assigned the greatest spoils and choice of the prizes to Rorik, by which he gained a nearer place in his love. Through his friendship with Rorik, he wooed and married his daughter Gerutha, who bore him a son, Amleth.

Feng was inflamed with jealousy at such good fortune, and resolved to thwart his brother by treason, for virtue is not safe even from one's own relatives. And when an opportunity to murder him appeared, his gory hand satisfied the blood-lust of his soul. Then he added incest to fratricide by taking possession of his slaughtered brother's wife, for he who gives himself to one crime soon falls downhill into the next; so one sin leads on to another.

Then he covered the atrocity of the deed with such bold artifice as to excuse his crime through a pretense of good will, and colored over the fratricide with a pious front. He said that Gerutha, though she was of such gentleness that she would not have done anyone the slightest harm, had suffered her husband's most vehement hate, and Feng had slain his brother to save her, because it seemed shameful to him that a very gentle and unspiteful woman should endure the heavy scorn of her husband. And his words did not fail to persuade, for a lie is easily believed at court, where favors are sometimes conferred upon fools and honor upon slanderers. Feng did not even withhold his murderer's hands from disgraceful embraces, pursuing both of his impious deeds with equal guilt.

II
AMLETH FEIGNS MADNESS

AMLETH SAW THIS, and to prevent arousing his uncle's suspicion through any show of prudence, he took on an appearance of stupidity and extreme infirmity of mind, and by this sort of guile hid his designs while also protecting his safety. Each day he stayed at his mother's house in a filthy torpor. Throwing his body on the ground, he would splash himself with grunge and dirt. The befouled color of his face and his grime-caked appearance signified a ridiculous and foolish insanity. All that he said was of a piece with madness; all that he did exhibited a profound lethargy. In brief, one would not have called him a man of any kind, but a monster made laughable by lunatic fortune.

Sometimes, he would sit at the fire and scoop up the cinders in his hands, to make wooden hooks and harden them in the flame. The ends of these he shaped into certain barbs, by which they would hold more tightly to their fastenings. When anyone asked what he was doing, he replied that he was preparing sharp spears to revenge his father. This response met with not a little mockery, because everyone derided the vanity of the ridiculous work. Yet afterwards it aided his purpose.

This craftiness aroused the first suspicion of his subtlety among the more intelligent observers, for this aptitude in a minor art suggested the hidden ability of a craftsman. And one whose hand had acquired such skillful artistry could not be thought dull of mind.

Lastly, he always watched over the heap of flame-sharpened sticks with the most exact care. Some claimed, therefore, that a nimble mind was enclosed behind this pretext of dullness, and that he hid a profound purpose behind a guise of stupidity. According to them, his cunning could be effectively discovered if a voluptuous woman were ever sent to him in a secret place. She could provoke his mind with the allurements of love, since nature runs so heedless into sensuality that it cannot be artfully dissembled. So if he were feigning idleness, he would, given the opportunity, submit at once to the compulsions of lust. Men were therefore hired to lead the youth on horseback into distant parts of the forest and there beset him with that kind of temptation.

One of Amleth's appointed followers, a foster-brother of his who still respected their common upbringing, happened to be present among these men. Because he placed the memory of their past fellowship before his present orders, he was eager to warn and not to entrap him, for he never doubted that Amleth would suffer the worst if he displayed any sign of intelligence, especially if he performed the act of love in the open.

This was also plain to Amleth himself, so when he was asked to mount a horse, he placed himself with his back turned to the horse's neck, looking down the tail.

Then he proceeded to place the reins around the tail just as if he would use that part to control the pace of the rushing horse. By this clever thinking he eluded his uncle's trick and defeated the treachery. It was a ridiculous enough spectacle to see the horse run on unbridled with the rider directing its tail.

When, passing through a thicket, Amleth came across a wolf, his comrades told him that a colt had run by. He replied that "There are too few of that kind in Feng's army," so that by a reserved but witty kind of invocation, he cursed his uncle's riches. When they construed that he had answered prudently, he declared that he had spoken carefully, so that he would not seem to lie about any point, for he wished to be thought a stranger to falsehood, and mixed subtlety with plainness so that his words would be true, yet no mark of truth would reveal the extent of his shrewdness.

Likewise, as he passed the beach, his companions, finding the rudder of a wrecked ship, said they had found an enormous knife. He said, "It was right for such a huge ham to be cut by this," meaning in fact that the immensity of the sea was proportionate to the size of the rudder. Again, passing the sand hills, they asked him to look at the "grains," meaning the sand. He replied that it had been ground down by the storms of the breaking ocean. When his companions admired his answer, he again declared that he had spoken shrewdly.

Then they intentionally left him alone so that he might take greater courage in the act of lust. He came upon the woman, whom his uncle had sent to an obscure place, as if by chance. He would have ravished her, but his foster-brother signaled him about the plot by a secret kind of sign. For he had considered what would be the most fitting way to play the prompter and avert the young man's perilous wantonness, and he attached a piece of straw that he had found on the ground to the underside of a gnat's tail as it flew past. He then drove the fly into the place where he knew Amleth to be; and by doing so, he did a great service to the reckless youth, for Amleth construed the message with no less prudence than his foster-brother had sent it.

When Amleth, in his curiosity, noticed the fly and the straw stuck to its tail, he understood that it was a secret warning of deceit. Alarmed by suspicion of the plot, he took hold of the woman and dragged her off to a distant marsh in order to have his desire more safely. Then, after they had slept together, he solemnly implored her not to tell anyone what had happened. She granted her silence as eagerly as he requested it, because their common education and early upbringing had brought Amleth and the girl into great intimacy since childhood.

And so he went home, and when the others asked teasingly if he had indulged in his pleasure, he confessed that he had ravished the girl. When asked again where he had done it and what he had used for a pillow, he said he had rested on the hoof of a beast of burden, on a coxcomb, and also on the panels of the ceiling (for when he was first giving in to temptation, he had gathered bits of all these things in order to avoid lying). These words roused much loud laughter from those present, although the joke had taken nothing but truth from the story.

And the girl, when asked about what happened, denied that she had done any such thing. And indeed, her denial was more easily believed when no witnesses to the deed were found. Then the one who had marked the gadfly as a sign, to show Amleth that he owed his salvation to his craftiness, declared that he had recently been particularly devoted to him. The young man's reply was apt: not to appear unmindful of the informer's merits, Amleth said that a certain bearer of straw had flown past his eye carrying a chaff fixed to its posterior. Even as these words raised laughter among the others, their prudence delighted Amleth's friend.

III
AMLETH CONFRONTS HIS MOTHER AND KILLS FENG'S SPY

WITH ALL OF THEM DEFEATED, unable to break the bolt of the young man's industry, one of Feng's friends (abounding with more presumption than wisdom) said Amleth's genius was inextricable, and that his cleverness could not be unveiled by any usual type of scheme. Indeed, his vigilance was too great to be overwhelmed by slight investigations. Indeed, the many sides of his cunning could not be borne out by any single test. And so he said that his own higher sensibilities had found a subtler course of inquiry, easy to enact and effective for the present investigation. Feng was to purposely depart, claiming to be on some great business. Then Amleth would be enclosed in a room with his mother, with a man hired beforehand who, unknown to either party, would place himself in a hidden part of the room, and would listen attentively to what passed between them. If the son had wisdom, he would not hesitate to speak to his mother's ears, nor would he greatly fear to trust the faith of the one who had born him. Likewise the counselor eagerly offered himself to be minister of the investigation, so as not to seem more ardent as the author of the plan than as its undertaker. Feng was delighted by the idea, and departed under pretense of a long journey.

Now the counselor went quietly to the room where Amleth was closed in with his mother, and lay hidden beneath the straw. But Amleth had a remedy for the treachery: since he feared to be overheard by some spy, he fell at first to his usual inept practices: he began crowing like a loud rooster, beat his arms like the flapping of wings, climbed up on the straw, and began to fling his body, leaping around, testing whether anything lay hidden there. And when he felt a heap beneath his feet, he stabbed the place with his sword and skewered the concealed man. Then he dragged him from his hiding place, killed him, cut his body into pieces, cooked it in boiling water, and hurled it into the open sewer to be devoured by the hogs, strewing the rotten mud with his miserable limbs.

One he had eluded the treachery, he returned to the room. When his mother began to weep in front of Amleth and sent up a great, lamenting wail for his foolishness, he said, "Disgraceful woman! Do you wish to conceal your heavy guilt with false lamenting? Have you not, as lascivious as a whore, entered a criminal, and detestable form of marriage, and wound yourself in the incestuous embrace of your husband's murderer? And do you fawn with obscene charms of blandishments upon him who killed the father of your son? Thus indeed do mares join with those who defeat their mates; this is the nature of brutes that go wantonly among diverse partners. You have followed their example and abolished your first husband's memory."

"But I do not lightly wear this mask of stupidity, for I do not doubt that he who stamped out his brother would revel in the same cruelty against his other relatives. And so it is better to take on the bearing of idiocy than of wisdom, and to shift into the guard of safety by an appearance of extreme delirium. Yet the lust for my father's revenge endures in my soul, though I lie in wait for the best occasion, and await an opportunity. Each thing must be done in its time. Against a dark and cruel mind, it is best to use higher paths of thought. It is superfluous for you to lament my foolishness, you who would do more rightly to bewail your own ignominy. You must weep for the vice of your own mind, not that of another. As for the rest, see to it that you hold your tongue." By such reproof, he restored his tattered mother to the path of virtue, and taught her to prefer the flames of the past to the allurements of the present.

When Feng returned, he could not find the man who

had devised the treacherous espionage. He looked for him long and carefully, but no one could say that he had seen him anywhere. Amleth too was jokingly asked if he had found any trace of him. He replied that the man had gone into the sewer, fallen through its bottom, drowned in the great deluge of mud, and been devoured by the swine who had come together underneath. Though these words confessed the express truth, all of the hearers laughed at them, since they appeared senseless.

IV
THE JOURNEY TO BRITAIN

FENG NOW SUSPECTED beyond question that Amleth was full of deceit, so he determined to kill his own stepson. But he quaked to do it for fear of his wife and also for Amleth's grandfather Rorik. So he decided that the king of Britain should do the deed, for Feng thought he could pretend innocence by having Amleth killed by the hand of another. So because he desired to hide his savageness, he preferred to inculpate his friend rather than bring infamy on himself.

Upon his departure, Amleth secretly told his mother to hang the royal court with woven knots, and after a year to give Amleth a false funeral. At that time, he promised, he would return. Two of Feng's agents set out with him, carrying with them a letter engraved on wood (for that was once a common type of writing). The letter commanded the king of the Britons to execute the young man who was sent over to him. While the agents were sleeping, Amleth searched their belongings and found the letter. Upon reading the orders, he erased the writing and substituted new writing on the surface, which altered the mandate so that its condemnation fell upon his companions. But he was not content only to shift the sentence of death from himself and lay the punishment on others. Endorsing the entreaty with the false signature of Feng, he requested the king of Britain to give his daughter in marriage to the wise young man who was being sent to him.

When they came to Britain, the legates went to the king and gave him the letter, thinking it an instrument of another man's doom, though it was really a herald of death to themselves. The king concealed what was in the letter and treated them with kind hospitality.

Then Amleth scorned the whole regal feast as if it were common food and shunned many dishes with a strange abstinence, avoiding the drinks no less than the food. All were amazed that a young foreigner would loathe the refined delicacies of the king's table and the treat the luxurious banquet they had prepared as if it were some rustic plate. At the end of the feast, while the king was sending his friends to rest, he saw to it that a certain man was sent into the sleeping-room to listen in secret to the night-time conversations of his guests.

When Amleth's companions asked him why he had abstained from the last night's meal as if it were poison, he said the bread was sprinkled with impure blood, that there was a taste of iron in the drink, and that the meats smelled of a human corpse and were corrupt with the stink of death. He also added that the king had the eyes of a slave, and that the queen had behaved like a bondmaid in three ways. In this manner, he reviled his host with even harsher insults than the banquet. His companions soon reproached him for the previous infirmity of his mind, and began to insult him with many petulant jokes, since he found fault with excellent and worthy things, and since he shamefully attacked an exemplary king and a cultured woman, spattering praiseworthy people with an extremely shameful reproach.

When the king heard of these things from the attendant, he declared that the one who could say such things had either superhuman wisdom or foolishness, for he grasped in these few words the full height of Amleth's workings. Then he called his steward and asked where he had gotten the bread. When the steward said it had been made by the household baker, the king likewise asked where the grain had been grown, from which it was made, and whether any sign of human carnage could be seen there. He responded that nearby was a field littered with the ancient bones of slain men, and which still bore the signs of the past massacre. He said he had planted the field himself in the spring in hopes that it would yield a more fruitful harvest than the others, and so he did not know if the bread had taken some rankness from the blood.

When the king heard this, he realized that Amleth had spoken the truth and so he sought to find where the lard had been brought from. The steward avouched that his pigs had been negligently allowed to stray from their keeping and had fed on the rotten corpse of a thief, and that perhaps this had given their pork a corrupt savor.

When the king found that Amleth had been right on this point, he inquired as to what liquor had been mixed with the drink. When he discovered it had been brewed of water and meal, he had the place of the spring shown to him and began digging deep in the ground. There he found many rusted swords, whose scent, it was thought, had tainted the spring waters. Others maintain that Amleth had denounced the drink because while he was drinking it, he found some bees that had fed on the guts of a dead man, and the contamination had emerged in the taste, which before had been lodged in the honeycombs.

The king saw by this that Amleth had correctly named the causes of the evil taste, and since he realized that the ignoble eyes for which Amleth had censured him pertained to some error in his birth, he met with his mother in secret and asked who his father had been. She said she had submitted to no one but the king, but when he threatened to have the truth from her by trial, she told him that he was the child of a slave. By the evidence of this confession the king understood the mystery of Amleth's reproach to his origin.

Though he was ashamed of the lowness of his station, he was so delighted by the wisdom of the young man that he asked why he had sullied the queen by saying she had acted like a slave. But even while it pained him that his wife's courtliness had been insulted in the midnight conversation of a guest, he discovered that she was the daughter of a handmaid. For Amleth said he had seen three blotches of servility upon her: first, because she covered her head with a mantle as handmaids do; second, because she lifted her gown when she walked; and third, because she had picked the remains of food stuck in the cracks of her teeth with a splinter, and then chewed it. He also reported that her mother had been taken into slavery from captivity, so that she was base in her birth as well as her habits.

The king venerated Amleth's wisdom as if it were an oracle, gave him his daughter in marriage, and embraced his words like the testament of heaven. Then, to fulfill his friend's request, he hanged Amleth's companions on the following day. Amleth pretended to be offended to the soul by this favor, so the king compensated him with gold, which Amleth then melted secretly in a fire and poured into two hollow sticks.

V
THE REVENGE OF AMLETH

AFTER STAYING A YEAR with the king, he took his leave to depart and returned home, taking nothing of his kingly wealth with him except the sticks that held the gold. Once he landed in Jutland, he exchanged his recent appearance for his old façade of foolishness, which he had used for honorable ends. When the grime-covered Amleth entered the banquet hall where his own funeral was being celebrated, he put everyone into great amazement, since he had been rumored dead.

At last, horror gave way to mirth as the guests laughingly rebuked each other that the man should appear alive whose funeral they were celebrating as if he were dead. When they asked him about his companions, he displayed the sticks he was carrying and said, "Here are they both." He said this both truly and jestingly, because this speech, though most considered it vain, did not depart from the truth, since Amleth's words pointed to the compensation he had received for the dead men as a figure of the men themselves.

Then, in order to heighten the guests' mirth, he joined with the cupbearers and busily poured the drinks. And to keep his loose garments from hindering his walk, he girded his sword on his side and drew it frequently, intentionally pricking his fingers with its point until the bystanders had the sword and the sheath struck through with an iron nail. Also, to assist the workings of his plot, he went to the noblemen and filled their cups over and over with the drink until they were too drunk to stand, and so went to sleep in the palace, making their beds on whatever spot they had been reveling.

Seeing that they were prepared for his plan, he now knew the opportunity for his purpose. He took out the stakes he had prepared so long before and then entered the building, where the noblemen lay all across the floor, belching in their drunkenness. Then he cut down the cords that held the hangings his mother had made, which covered both the inner and outer parts of the royal court. He threw this over the sleeping men and used the crooked stakes to tie them up so inextricably that no one lying under, however strongly he tried, could manage to raise himself. After that, he set fire to the palace. The flames grew, spread the pyre through the whole building, consumed the palace, and burned them all even as they lay locked in sleep or struggled vainly to rise.

Going from there to the bedchamber, where Feng had earlier been led by his followers, he snatched a sword that chanced to be hanging on the bed and put his own in its place. Then he woke his uncle, told him his nobles were perishing in the fire, and that Amleth was here, assisted by his hooks, and burning to enact the long due penalty for his father's murder. Hearing this, Feng leapt down from the bed, but could not find his own sword. As he vainly tried to draw the foreign one, Amleth cut him down.

Oh, brave man and worthy of eternal fame, who, wisely armed with a pretense of folly, buried a wisdom beyond human understanding in a wonderful disguise of ineptitude, and who not only achieved his own preservation by this cunning, but also the means to avenge his father! And so, by cleverly preserving his safety and mightily revenging his father, he has left us in doubt whether to praise him most for his bravery or his wisdom.

VI
AMLETH'S SPEECH TO THE JUTES
(GESTA DANORUM, BOOK IV, CHAPTER 1)

WITH THE OVERTHROW of his stepfather complete, Amleth feared to display his deed to the fickle judgment of the people, so he decided to lay in hiding until he had learned the inclinations of the disorderly rabble. So in the morning, the neighborhood, which had seen the inferno at night, desired to know the cause of the remarkable fire, and found the royal palace collapsed into ashes. Searching through its smoldering ruins, they found nothing but the shapeless remains of charred bodies. The ravenous flames had devoured all to such a degree that there remained not even a shred by which the cause of so great a disaster might be understood. The body of Feng was also seen, pierced by iron among the bloody spoils.

Some of the people were struck with a wounded indignation, others by grief, but still others experienced a closeted joy. While some were lamenting the fate of their ruler, others rejoiced that the fratricide's tyranny was laid to rest. So the destruction of the king was met with mixed opinions from those who saw it.

When the people were quiet, Amleth took courage to leave his hiding place and called together those in whom he knew the memory of his father to remain. Then he went out to the assembly, where he spoke in this way:

"Noble sirs, do not be moved by the show of the present calamity, not if you are moved by the miserable end of Horvendile; do not be moved, I say, you for whom regal power and parental honor have been salvaged. You see before you the funeral of a fratricide, not a king. It was a more tragic sight indeed, when you saw your king wretchedly butchered by an iniquitous fratricide, unfit to be called brother. Your own eyes have looked compassionately on the mangled limbs of Horvendile; yourselves have seen his body wrecked by a forest of wounds. Who doubts that the atrocious butcher robbed him of life in order to strip the country of liberty? One hand hurled doom on him and slavery on you. Who then is such a madman, that he would prefer the cruelty of Feng to the piety of Horvendile? Remember with what benevolence Horvendile nurtured you, with what justice he fostered you, with what humanity he loved you. You will recall the gentlest of kings, the most just of fathers taken from you, a tyrant offered in his place, a fratricide as substitute, the country polluted with shame, a yoke imposed upon your necks, and the rights of liberty stripped away.

"And now, when all is finished, you see the culprit buried in his own crimes. The murderer of his own kindred has paid the price for his felonies. Who but a fool will consider this benefit as an injury? What sane person would pity the offender for having his own crime turned back on him? Who would weep for the killing of the bloodiest executioner, or lament the just destruction of the cruelest of tyrants? You see me before you, the author of this act; I indeed confess that I have pursued revenge both for father and for fatherland."

"I have done the work that ought also to have been done by your hands. What you should have done along with me I have accomplished alone, for I had no partner in such a blameless treason, nor did anyone aid me in the work. Although I knew that you would have given aid to this labor had I asked, since I knew that you have all preserved your love to your king and fidelity to your prince. But I wished to punish these beasts without your help. For I did not think that this burden should be laid on others' shoulders, since I believed my own were strong enough to carry it."

"I have cremated the other bodies; I left only Feng's carcass to be burned by your hands, on which at least you may fully satiate the desire of just revenge. Come together eagerly, erect a pyre, burn his impious body, bake his wicked joints, scatter the guilty ashes, and cast apart the hot-glowing coals; let no urn, no mound enclose the unnamable relics of his bones. Let no trace of the fratricide remain, no place in his country for his contaminated limbs, nor any vicinity to suck up his contagion; neither sea nor earth must be polluted by the company of his damned cadaver. I have done the rest; only this pious duty has been left to you: to follow the tyrant with this train, and lead the fratricide's funeral with this procession. It is not fit that even his ashes, which stripped the nation of liberty, should be covered by the soil of the fatherland."

"Why, furthermore, should I repeat my own sorrows, recount my calamities, rework my miseries, since you yourselves know them better than I? I, who have been hunted to death by my stepfather, despised by my mother, spat on by my friends, and have passed the years tearfully, I have led calamitous days and an uncertain life beset by fears and danger. In short, I have followed every season of my time in misery, and with the greatest adversity."

You have often sighed and whispered secretly among yourselves that since I was devoid of my wits, my father had no revenger, none to take vengeance on the fratricide. I saw this secret witness of your love, and knew from it that the memory of the king's murder had not left your minds. Whose breast is so hard and stony that my sufferings and labors do not bend him to compassion? You, whose hands are innocent of Horvendile's murder, pity me your nursling and be moved by my misfortunes. Take pity also on my wretched mother, and let us all rejoice that the shame of your former queen has been expunged, she who in her woman's weakness was made to endure the two shameful burdens of embracing her husband's brother as well as his murderer."

"And so, to hide my quest for vengeance, I concealed my intelligence and pretended to become listless; using an appearance of stupidity, I made a plan, which now lays open before your eyes to see; as for the great question of whether it was a success, and if it achieved its aim, I am content to leave you to judge. Now you yourselves must trample upon the ashes of the fratricide, lay scorn on his remains who defiled his murdered brother's wife unto utter disgrace, offended his lord, committed treason against his sovereign, subjected you to bitter tyranny, robbed you of liberty, and added incest to fratricide."

"With your noblest spirits uphold me, the minister of this just revenge; give homage to me, who have hungered for this holy reckoning, and restore me with your kind looks. I have erased the country's disgrace, snuffed my mother's shame, repulsed tyranny, stamped out the fratricide, and eluded my uncle's crafty hand with contrivances of my own. If he had lived, he would have added to his crimes in future days. I bewailed the injury done to my father and fatherland; I killed him who ruled you with atrocious hardness unfitting for a man."

Recognize the favor I have done you, honor my craftiness, and give me, if I have earned it, the crown; I have done a great deed for you, and I am a worthy successor to my father's power: not a fratricide, but the pious revenger of that crime and rightful heir to the throne. You are indebted to me for recovering the gift of liberty, shutting out the afflicter's rule, lifting the oppressor's yoke, shaking the fratricide's power, and trampling the scepter of tyranny. I have stripped you of slavery, clothed you with freedom, restored your pomp and glory, overthrown the tyrant, and vanquished the butcher. My payment is yours to give; you know what I have merited, and I ask you, by your virtue, to give me my reward."

The young man's speech touched everyone's hearts; some were moved to compassion, others even to tears. And when the weeping subsided, they all proclaimed him king in an instant, since indeed, all of them lay their hope on his wisdom, since he had arranged such a great work with the profoundest industry, and completed it with incredible industry. Many were seen wondering how he had concealed his subtle plan for such a long time.

VII
AMLETH'S RETURN TO BRITAIN AND MISSION TO SCOTLAND

WHEN HE HAD FINISHED his duties in Denmark, Amleth loaded three ships with bounty and returned to Britain to see his father and his wife. He also took the most eminent youths into his employment and dressed them exquisitely so that even as he had once worn a despicable habit, he now gave magnificent preparation to all things and changed his former dedication to poverty into an outlay of luxury. He also commanded a shield to be made for him, and ordered depictions made on it of the whole story of his deeds since earliest childhood, all adorned with exquisite designs. By carrying this shield as a record of his virtues, he enlarged his fame all the more.

On it were seen depictions of Horvendile's slaughter, Feng's fratricide and incest, the infamous uncle, the ridiculous nephew, the crooked shapes of the staves, the stepfather's suspicion, the stepson's dis-simulation, the various temptations procured, the woman brought to trick him, the gaping wolf, the discovery of the rudder, the crossing of the sand, the entering of the woods, the straw stuck to the fly, the young man warned by this signal, and his secret congress with the maiden after eluding their companions. And there was still more to see: a picture of the palace, the queen present with her son, the killing of the spy, the cooking of the corpse, the morsels dropped into the sewer, thrown out to the swine, and the limbs scattered in the mud and left for the animals to consume. Also to be seen was how Amleth discovered the secret of his slumbering companions, how he erased the old letter and exchanged it with a new one, how he despised the banquet and scorned the drink, how he accused the face of the king, and pointed out the queen's low behavior. The hanging of the legates was also depicted, as was the young man's wedding, the voyage back to Denmark, the banquet to celebrate Amleth's funeral, Amleth answering the guests' questions by displaying the stick in place of his companions, the young man playing the cupbearer and intentionally pricking his fingers with the drawn sword, the nail struck through the sword, the festivities growing loud, the dances accelerating, the hangings thrown down on the sleepers, then fastened around them by the tightly woven hooks as they lay, the house set on fire, the guests cremated, the fire-wasted palace collapsing, Amleth going to Feng's bedroom, stealing the sword, replacing it with the useless one, and the king killed by his stepson's hand with the point of his own sword. A skilled artisan painted all these things on his battle-shield with refined art, imitating true things in his figures, and encompassing real deeds with his outlines. And Amleth's companions, to appear all the more splendid, also carried shields of gold.

The king of Britain received them kindly and served

them with rich and royal ceremony. As they feasted, he asked eagerly whether Feng continued to live and prosper. His son-in-law told him that he asked vainly after the health of a man who had perished by the sword. The king poured forth questions trying to know who had killed Feng, and learned that the messenger of his death was also its author. This news struck the king in his secret heart for he realized he was bound by an ancient vow to avenge Feng, since he and Feng had long before resolved by a common pact that each of them would avenge the other. And so the king was torn on the one hand between his duty to his daughter and love for his son-in-law, and on the other by love for his friend, and also by the firmness of the oath and sacredness of their mutual pledge, which would be impious to violate. In the end, he put his family in contempt in favor of his sworn faith, and his soul turned to revenge, placing sanctity before affinity. But since it was thought a sin to violate the sacred duties of hospitality, he chose to execute his revenge through another man's hand, so that he could advance an appearance of innocence over his secret guilt.

So he masked his designs with favors and obscured his harmful purpose with an artfully studied benevolence. And since his wife had recently died of an illness, he asked Amleth to take up the task of finding him a new wife, saying how wholly pleased he was by Amleth's personal wisdom. He said that a certain woman ruled in Scotland, whom he vigorously wished to marry. For he knew she was unmarried, not only because of her chastity, but also because of her arrogant cruelty, for the woman hated her suitors and had always leveled the ultimate punishment on her lovers, so that not even one of the many remained who had not paid for his impudence with his head.

So Amleth set forth. Although he had been ordered on a perilous mission, he never shirked his obedience to a commanded duty, but trusting partly in his own servants and partly in the king's retainers, he went into Scotland. When he was not far from the queen's home, he went to a meadow beside the road to rest his horses, and there, pleased by the look of the place, he thought of resting, and, with the pleasant murmuring of the stream provoking his desire to sleep, he appointed men to watch the spot from a distance. When the queen heard of this, she sent out ten young men to spy on the strangers' approach and their equipment. One of them, who was quick-witted, snuck past the guards, then steadily approached, and removed Amleth's shield, which happened to have been laid beneath his head before he slept. He removed the shield so gently that even though Amleth was laying on it, the spy did not disturb his sleep or awaken any of the soldiers, for he desired to give his mistress not only his report, but also to proffer some evidence of his exploit. With equal guile he also stole the letter entrusted to Amleth from the satchel in which it was being kept.

When he brought these things to the queen, she examined the shield carefully and from the attached letters deduced the entire story, and knew that a man was at hand who, trusting in his own precise and prudent plot, had punished his uncle for his father's murder. When she also examined the letter containing the petition for her hand, she erased all of the writing, because she utterly abhorred marriage to the old and hungered for the embrace of the young. But she wrote a mandate in its place seeming to be sent from the king of Britain to herself and signed as before with his name and title, in which she pretended that she was asked to marry the bearer. She also saw to it that the letter mentioned the deeds that she discovered from the shield so that it would seem that the shield and the letter confirmed one another. Then she told the men whom she had sent out before to now carry back the shield and replace the letter, using the same kind of trick on Amleth that she had learned he used in fooling his companions.

Meanwhile, Amleth discovered that the shield had been stolen from under his head, and so he purposely shut his eyes and cleverly pretended to sleep in hopes of reclaiming by a false slumber what he had lost in a real one. He thought that the thief's first success would incline him to attempt another deception. And his judgment held true. Indeed, as the spy came secretly, desiring to replace the shield and letter in their original place, Amleth leapt forward, took him captive, and bound him in chains. Then he awoke his companions and went to the queen's home. He greeted her in his father-in-law's person and offered her the letter with the king's seal. When Hermutrude (for that was the queen's name) took and read it, she spoke great words in praise of Amleth's labor and industry and said Feng had deserved his just punishment, but that Amleth himself had used an unfathomable genius to achieve a feat beyond human estimation, because he had not only wisely devised the revenge of his father's doom and his mother's adultery, but had also used outstanding probity to take over the kingdom of the man whose constant plots he had endured.

She was therefore amazed that a man of such erudite knowledge could have made one singular error in his marriage, for though he almost transcended mortality by his reputation, he now seemed to have lapsed into an obscure and ignoble match. Indeed, his wife was the child of slaves, even though fortune had adorned them with royal honors. The queen said that in seeking out a marriage, it is not prudent to esteem the glitter of a woman's beauty, but that of her descent. And so, if Amleth were to seek for a match properly, he would esteem lineage and not be taken in by appearance, which was a strong incentive to temptation, although its hollow colors had often smudged the whiteness of many men's purity.

But a woman there was equal to him in nobility, whom he could take up, for she herself was neither poor in possession nor humble in blood and was worthy of his embraces, since he neither bettered her in royal estate nor exceeded her in ancestral glory. Indeed she was a queen, but if her sex had not prevented it, she could be called a king; or rather (which is truer) whomever she deemed worthy of her bed was become a king, for she gave her throne together with her embrace. Thus her scepter accompanied her hand and her hand her scepter. And it was no meager gift for her to offer her love, she who with other men had followed her refusal with the sword. She begged him therefore to transfer his courting to her, turn over to her his marriage vow, and learn to favor lineage over beauty. Saying these things, she fell to embracing him.

Amleth was delighted by the maiden's courtly speech and kissed her in return, repaid her tight embraces, and proclaimed that what pleased her pleased him. Then they held a banquet; friends were summoned, the noblemen brought together, and the marriage performed. When these things were done, he returned to Britain with his bride and with a strong retinue of Scots commanded to follow close behind, so that he could use their help against the various dangers on his way.

VIII
THE DEATH OF AMLETH

As he was returning, the daughter of the king of Britain, to whom he was still married, ran to meet him. Although she bitterly complained that she was wronged to have a mistress favored over her, still she said it would be unfitting for her to bear him more hate as an adulterer than love as a husband, and she would not turn so far against him as to keep silence about a deception that she knew was intended against him, since she had a son as a seal of their marriage, the respect of whom at least ought to have stirred the mother to love for her spouse.

"For he," she said, "might hate his mother's replacement, but I will love her; no calamity shall put out my fire for you, no spite extinguish it, or keep me from disclosing the sinister designs against you and unfolding the plots that I have discovered. So think your father-in-law a danger to you, since you have reaped the crop of your embassy for yourself, and eluded the wish of the man who sent you by obdurately usurping all of his harvest." With this speech she showed herself nearer in love to her husband than to her father.

As she said these things, the king of Britain came forth and, embracing his son-in-law closely but without love, received him at a banquet to conceal his plan of deceit behind a show of openhandedness. Amleth, knew of the fraud and disguised his fear, and taking a retinue of two hundred horsemen and putting on a coat of mail beneath his shirt, obeyed the invitation, for he preferred the danger of complying with the king's deception than retreating in shame, for he valued honor to such an extent as to observe it in all things.

When he rode up close, the king attacked him under the porch of his folding doors and would have lanced him through with his javelin had not a hard coat of mail repelled the blade. Having suffered a slight wound, Amleth took himself to the place where he had ordered the Scottish host to wait on duty, and sent back to the king his new wife's spy, the same man whom he had captured, to testify that he himself had in stealth taken the letter intended for his mistress from the satchel where it was kept. In this way he would shift the charge back on Hermutrude and carefully excuse and absolve Amleth from the accusation of treason.

The king made no delay in pursuing Amleth in his flight and deprived him of most of his troops, so that on the following day, Amleth, intent on fighting for his life and entirely desperate in his strength to resist, tried to increase the apparent numbers of his troops by setting up stakes to prop up the dead bodies of some of his companions. He tied the bodies of some to nearby stones, and placed others on horses like living men, with none of their armor removed, and arranged them in line and wedge formation just as if they were going to battle. There were as many in the host of the dead as in the army of the living. It was a ponderous sight indeed as the dead were drawn into battle, the deceased mustered to the contest. The plan served Amleth well, for those figures of the dead looked like an immense army in the sunlight, since those dead, insensate shapes restored the full number of the army so well that nothing seemed diminished from their troop by the previous day's carnage.

At the sight of the army, the terrified Britons fled running from the battle, overcome by the dead men whom they had defeated in life. I do not know whether to think that this victory was won more by cunning or good fortune. And the king, running tardily away, was cut down by the charging Danes. The victorious Amleth took great plunder, seizing the spoils of Britain, and returned with his wives to his homeland.

(GESTA DANORUM, BOOK IV, CHAPTER 2)

Meanwhile, Rorik had died, and Wiglek came to the throne. He harassed Amleth's mother with every manner of impudence, deprived her of all her possessions, and claimed her son had defrauded the king of Leire, who had the right to give and take privileges of honor, and that he had usurped the throne of Jutland. Amleth suffered this with such mildness that he appeared to repay the calumny with kindness by giving Wiglek the most splendid prizes of his victory. But afterwards he seized an occasion of taking revenge, and, revealing himself from the shadows as an open foe, made battle on Wiglek and defeated him. He drove Fialler, the governor of Skaäne into exile, and the story goes that Fialler withdrew to a place called Udensakre, which is unknown to our people.

After that, Wiglek was restored by forces of Skaäne and Zealand, and sent legates challenging Amleth to war. Amleth's marvelous wisdom perceived that he was thrown between two dangerous currents, one of which entailed disgrace, and the other danger. He knew if he accepted the challenge, he would certainly jeopardize his life, but if he refused, he would suffer probation as a soldier. Yet Amleth's soul was ever fixated on excellence, and so his desire of saving honor and his urgent yearning for acclaim blunted and conquered his fear of destruction, for he would not let the unstained brightness of his glory be tainted by a cowardly evasion of fate. He also realized that almost as great a gulf lay between an ignoble life and a glorious death as that which is known to lie between dignity and disgrace.

But he was so enfettered by love for Hermutrude that he carried a more engrained anxiety in his soul for her future widowhood than for his own death, and before going to war, he sought with all zeal to find how he could settle on a second husband for her. But Hermutrude professed to have the courage of a man, and pledged that she would not desert him even in battle, saying it was a detestable woman who feared to be joined with her husband in death. But she scarcely obeyed this singular promise, for when Amleth was slain by Wiglek in battle in Jutland, she willingly yielded herself to be the conqueror's bounty and bride.

Thus all women's vows are stripped away by the shifting of fortune and dissolved by the changing of the times, and the faith of their souls, clinging to a slippery footing, is weakened by casual chances, for it makes promises easily, pursues them as sluggishly, is roped in by all manner of lustful urges, and, always desiring to pursue new things, forgets the old and flies apart with heaving and impetuous desire.

This was the end of Amleth, who, had he been blessed by fortune as much as by nature, would have rivaled the gods in glory, and exceeded the labors of Hercules by his noble works. A field lies in Jutland famous for his tomb and his name. Wiglek had a long and peaceful rule, and died of a sickness.

THE HYSTORIE OF HAMBLET

LONDON:
Imprinted by *Richard Bradocke*, for *Thomas Paiuer*,
and are to be sole at his shop in Corne-hill,
neere to the Royall Exchange.

1608.

The Argument

It is not at this present, neither yet a small time since, that envy reigning in the worlde hath in such sort blinded men, that without respect of consanguinitie, friendship, or favour whatsoever, they forget themselves so much as that they spared not to defile their hands with the blood of those men, who by law and all right they ought chiefly to defend and cherish. For what other impression was it that entered into Romulus heart, when, under pretence of I know not what lawe, he defiled his hands with the blood of his owne brother, but the abhominable vice of desire to raigne? which, if in all the accurrences, prosperities, and circum-stances thereof, it were well wayed and considered, I know not any man that had not rather live at his ease, and privately without charge, then, being feared and honored of all men, to beare all the charge and burden upon his shoulders; to serve and please the fantasies of the common people; to live continually in feare, and to see himself exposed to a thousand occasions of danger, and most commonly assailed and spoiled when hee thinkes verily to hold Fortune as slave to his fantasies and will, and yet buyes such and so great misery for the vaine and fraile pleasures of this world, with the losse of his own soule; making so large a measure of his conscience, that it is not once mooved at any murther, treason, deceit, nor wicked nes whatsoever he committed, so the way may be opened and made plaine unto him, whereby hee may attaine to that miserable felicitie, to command and governe a multitude of men (as I said of Romulus), who, by a most abhominable action, prepared himselfe a way to heaven (but not by vertue). The ambitious and seditious Orator of Rome supposed the degrees and step to heaven, and the wayes to vertue, to consist in the treasons, ravishments, and massacres committed by him that first layd the foundations of that citty. And not to leave the hystories of Rome, what, I pray you, incited Ancius Martinus to massacre Tarquin the Elder, but the desire of raigning as a king, who before had bin the onely man to move and solicite the saide Tarquinius to bereave the right heires and inheriters thereof? What caused Tarquinius the Proud traiterously to imbrue his hands in the blood of Servius Tullius, his father in law, but onely that fumish and unbridled desire to be commander over the cittie of Rome? which practise never ceased nor discontinued in the said principall cittie of the empire, as long as it was governed by the greatest and wisest personages chosen and elected by the people; for therein have been seen infinite numbers of seditions, troubles, pledges, ransommings, confis-cations and massacres, onely proceeding from this ground and principle, which entereth into mens hearts, and maketh them covetous and desirous to be heads and rulers of a whole common wealth. And after the people were deprived of that libertie of election, and that the empire became subject to the pleasure and fantasie of one man, commanding al the rest, I pray you peruse their bookes, and read diligently their hystories, and do but looke into the meanes used by the most part of their kings and emperours to attaine to such power and authoritie, and you shall see how poysons, massacres, and secret murthers, were the meanes to push them forwards that durst not openly attempt it, or else could not compasse to make open warres. And for that the Hystory (which I pretend to shew unto you) is chiefly grounded upon treason, committed by one brother against the other, I will not erre far out of the matter; thereby desiring to shew you, that it is and hath been a thing long since practised and put in use by men, to spill the blood of their neerest kinsmen and friends to attaine to the honour of being great and in authoritie; and that there hath bin some, that being impatient of staying till their just time of succession, have hastened the death of their owne parents: as Absolon would have done to the holy king David, his father; and as wee read of Domitian, that poysoned his brother Titus, the most curtious and liberall prince that ever swayed the empire of Rome. And God knowes we have many the like examples in this our time, where the sonne conspired against the father; for that Sultan Zelin, emperour of Turkes, was so honest a man, that fearing Bajazeth, his father, would die of his naturall death, and that thereby he should have stayd too long for the empire, bereaved him of his life; and Sultan Soliman, his successor, although he attempted not any thing against his father, yet being mooved with a certaine feare to bee deposed from his emperie, and bearing a hatred to Mustapha, his son (incited thereunto by Rustain Bassa, whom the Jewes, enemies to the yong prince, had by gifts procured thereunto), caused him to be strangled with a bowe string, without hearing him (that never had offended his father) once speake to justifie his innocencie. But let us leave the Turkes, like barbarians as they are, whose throne is ordinarily established by the effusion of the blood of those that are neerest of kindred and consanguinitie to the empire, and consider what tragedies have bin plaid to the like effect in the memorie of our ancestors, and with what charitie and love the neerest kindreds and friends among them have bin intertained. One of the other, if you had not the hystories extant before you, if the memorie were not in a manner fresh, and known almost to every man, I would make a long discourse thereof; but things being so cleare and evident, the truth so much discovered, and the people almost, as it were, glutted with such treasons, I will omit them, and follow my matter, to shew you that, if the iniquitie of a brother caused his brother to loose his life, yet that vengeance was not long after delayed; to the end that traitors may know, although the punishment of their trespasses committed be stayed for awhile, yet that they may assure themselves that, without all doubt, they shal never escape the puisant and revenging hand of God; who being slow to anger, yet in the ende doth not faile to shew some signes and evident tokens of his fearefull judgement upon such as, forgetting their duties, shed innocent blood, and betray their rulers, whom they ought chiefly to honour, serve, and reverence.

THE PREFACE

ALTHOUGH in the beginning of this Hystorie I had determined not to have troubled you with any other matter than a hystorie of our owne time, having sufficient tragicall matter to satisfie the minds of men; but because I cannot wel discourse thereof without touching many personages whom I would not willingly displease, and partly because the argument that I have in hand, seemed unto me a thing worthy to bee offered to our French nobilitie, for the great and gallant accurrences therein set downe, I have somewhat strayed from my course, as touching the tragedies of this our age, and, starting out of France and over Neitherlanders countries, I have ventured to visit the hystories of Denmarke, that it may serve for an example of vertue and contentment to our nation (whom I specially seeke to please), and for whose satisfaction I have not left any flower whatsoever untasted, from whence I have not drawne the most perfect and delicate hony, thereby to bind them to my diligence herein; not caring for the ingratitude of the time present, that leaveth (as it were rejecteth) without recompence such as serve the common wealth, and by their travell and diligence honour their countrey, and illustrate the realme of France: so that oftentimes the fault proceeded rather from them, then from the great personages that have other affaires which withdraw them from things that seeme of small consequence. Withall, esteeming my selfe more than satisfied in this contentment and freedome with I now injoy, being loved

of the nobilitie, for whom I travell without grudging, favoured of men of learning and knowledge, for admiring
and reverencing them according to their worthinesse, and
honoured of the common people, of whom, although I
crave not their judgement, as not esteeming them of abili-
tie to eternize the name of a worthy man, yet I account
my selfe sufficiently happy to have attained to this felicitie, that few or no men refuse, or disdaine to reade my
workes, many admiring and wondering thereat; as there
are some that, provoked by envie, blame and condemne it.
To whom I confesse my selfe much bound and beholding,
for that by their meanes I am the more vigelant, and so
by my travell much more beloved and honored then ever I
was; which to mee is the greatest pleasure that I can injoy,
and the most abundant treasures in my coffers, where-
with I am more satisfied and contented then (if without
comparison) I enjoyed the greatest treasures in all Asia.
Now, returning to our matter, let us beginne to declare the
Hystorie.

CHAPTER I

*How Horvendile and Fengon were made Governours
of the Province of Ditmarse, and how Horvendile marryed
Geruth, the daughter to Roderick, chief K. of Denmark, by
whom he had Hamblet: and how after his marriage his
brother Fengon slewe him trayterously, and marryed his
brothers wife, and what followed.*

You must understand, that long time before the kingdome of Denmark received the faith of Jesus Christ, and imbraced the doctrin of the Christians, that the common people in those dayes were barbarous and uncivill, and their princes cruell, without faith or loyaltie, seeking nothing but murther, and deposing (or at the least) offending each other, either in honours, goods, or lives; not caring to ransome such as they tooke prisoners, but rather sacrificing them to the cruell vengeance naturally imprinted in their hearts: in such sort, that if ther were sometime a good prince or king among them, who beeing adorned with the most perfect gifts of nature, would adict himself to vertue, and use courtesie, although the people held him in admiration (as vertue is admirable to the most wicked) yet the envie of his neighbors was so great, that they never ceased untill that vertuous man were dispatched out of the world. King Rodericke, as then raigning in Denmarke, after hee had appeased the troubles in the countrey, and driven the Sweathlanders and Slaveans from thence, he divided the kindom into divers provinces, placing governours therein; who after (as the like happened in France) bare the names of Dukes, Marqueses, and Earls, giving the government of Jutie (at this present called Ditmarsse) lying upon the countrey of the Cimbrians, in the straight or narrow part of land that sheweth like a point or cape of ground upon the sea, which neithward bordereth upon the countrey of Norway, two valiant and warlike lords Horvendile and Fengon, sonnes to Gervendile, who likewise had beene governour of that province. Now the greatest honour that

men of noble birth could at that time win and obtaine,
was in exercising the art of piracie upon the seas, assayling
their neighbours, and the countries bordering upon them;
and how much the more they used to rob, pill, and spoyle
other provinces, and ilands far adjacent, so much the more
their honours and reputation increased and augmented:
wherin Horvendile obtained the highest place in his
time, beeing the most renouned pirate that in those dayes
scoured the seas and havens of the north parts: whose great
fame so mooved the heart of Collere, king of Norway, that
he was much grieved to heare that Horvendile surmount-
ing him in feates of armes, thereby obscuring the glorie
by him alreadie obtained upon the seas: (honor more than
covetousnesse of riches (in those dayes) being the reason
that provoked those barbarian princes to overthrow and
vanquish one the other, not caring to be slaine by the
handes of a victorious person). This valiant and hardy king
having challenged Horvendile to fight with him body to
body, the combate was by him accepted, with conditions,
that hee which should be vanquished should loose all the
riches he had in his ship, and that the vanquisher should
cause the body of the vanquished (that should bee slaine
in the combate) to be honourably buried, death being the
prise and reward of him that should loose the battaile: and
to conclude, Collere, king of Norway (although a valiant,
hardy, and couragious prince) was in the end vanquished
and slaine by Horvendile, who presently caused a tombe
to be erected, and therein (with all honorable obsequies
fit for a prince) buried the body of king Collere, according

to their auncient manner and superstitions in these dayes, and the conditions of the combate, bereaving the kings shippes of all their riches; and having slaine the kings sister, a very brave and valiant warriour, and over runne all the coast of Norway, and the Northern Ilands, returned home againe layden with much treasure, sending the most part thereof to his soveraigne, king Rodericke, thereby to procure his good liking, and so to be accounted one of the greatest favourites about his majestie.

The king, allured by those presents, and esteeming himselfe happy to have to valiant a subject, sought by a great favour and coutesie to make him become bounden unto him perpetually, giving him Geruth his daughter to his wife, of whom he knew Horvendile to bee already much inamored. And the more to honor him, determined himselfe in person to conduct her into Jutie, where the marriage was celebrated according to the ancient manner: and to be briefe, of this marriage proceeded Hamblet, of whom I intend to speake, and for his cause have chosen to renew this present hystorie.

Fengon, brother to this prince Horvendile, who [not] onely fretting and despighting in his heart at the great honor and reputation wonne by his brother in warlike affaires, but solicited and provoked by a foolish jealousie to see him honored with royall aliance, and fearing thereby to bee deposed from his part of the government, or rather desiring to be onely governour, thereby to obscure the memorie of the victories and conquests of his brother Horvendile, determined (whatsoever happened) to kill him; which hee effected in such sort, that no man once so much as suspected him, every man esteeming that from such and so firme a knot of alliance and consanguinitie there could proceed no other issue then the full effects of vertue and courtesie: but (as I sayd before) the desire of bearing soveraigne rule and authoritie respecteth neither blood nor amitie, nor caring for vertue, as being wholly without respect of lawes, or majestie devine; for it is not possible that hee which invadeth the countrey and taketh away the riches of an other man without cause or reason, should know or feare God. Was not this a craftie and sub-tile counsellor? but he might have thought that the mother, knowing her husbands case, would not cast her sonne into the danger of death. But Fengon, having secretly assem-bled certain men, and perceiving himself strong enough to execute his interprise, Horvendile his brother being at a banquet with his friends, sodainely set upon him, where he slewe him as traiterously, as cunningly he purged himselfe of so detestable a murther to his subjects; for that before he had any violent or bloody handes, or once committed parricide upon his brother, hee had incestuously abused his wife, whose honour hee ought as well to have sought and procured as traiterously he pursued and effected his destruction. And it is most certaine, that the man that abandoneth himselfe to any notorious and wicked action, whereby he becommeth a great sinner, he careth not to commit much more haynous and abhominable offences, and covered his boldnesse and wicked practise with so great subtiltie and policie, and under a vaile of meere sim-

plicitie, that beeing favoured for the honest love that he
bare to his sister in lawe, for whose sake, hee affirmed,
he had in that sort murthered his brother, that his sinne
found excuse among the common people and of the nobilitie was esteemed for justice: for that Geruth, being as
courteous a princesse as any then living in the north parts,
and one that had never once so much as offended any of
her subjects, either commons or courtyers, this adulterer
and infamous murtherer, slaundered his dead brother, that
hee would have slaine his wife, and that hee by chance
finding him upon the point ready to do it, in defence of
the lady had slaine him, bearing off the blows, which as
then he strooke at the innocent princesse, without any
other cause of malice whatsoever. Wherein hee wanted
no false witnesses to approove his act, which deposed in
like sort, as the wicked calumniator himselfe protested,
being the same persons that had born him company, and
were participants of his treason; so that insteed of pursuing him as a parricide and an incestuous person, al the
courtyers admired and flattered him in his good fortune,
making more account of false witnesses and detestable
wicked reporters, and more honouring the calumniators,
then they esteemed of those that seeking to call the matter in question, and admiring the vertues of the murthered
prince, would have punished the massacrers and bereav-
ers of his life. Which was the cause that Fengon, boldned
and incouraged by such impunitie, durst venture to couple
himselfe in marriage with her whom hee used as his concubine during good Horvendiles life, in that sort spot-

ting his name with a double vice, and charging his con-science with abhominable guilt, and two-fold impietie, as incestuous adulterie and parricide murther: and that the unfortunate and wicked woman, that had receaved the honour to bee the wife of one of the valiantest and wiseth princes in the north, imbased her selfe in such vile sort, as to falsifie her faith unto him, and which is worse, to marrie him, that had bin the tyranous murtherer of her lawfull husband; which made divers men thinke that she had beene the causer of the murther, thereby to live in her adultery without controle. But where shall a man finde a more wicked and bold woman, then a great parsonage once having loosed the bands of honor and honestie? This princesse, who at the first, for her rare vertues and court-esses was honored of al men and beloved of her husband, as soone as she once gave eare to the tyrant Fengon, forgot both the ranke she helde among the greatest names, and the dutie of an honest wife on her behalfe. But I will not stand to gaze and mervaile at women, for that there are many which seeke to blase and set them foorth, in which their writings they spare not to blame them all for the faults of some one, or few women. But I say, that either nature ought to have bereaved man of that opinion to ac-company with women, or els to endow them with such spirits, as that they may easily support the crosses they endure, without complaining so often and so strangely, seeing it is their owne beastlinesse that overthrowes them. For if it be so, that a woman is so imperfect a creature as they make her to be, and that they know this beast to bee so hard to bee tamed as they affirme, why then are they so foolish to preserve them, and so dull and brutish as to trust their deceitfull and wanton imbraceings. But let us leave her in this extreamitie of laciviousnesse, and proceed to shewe you in what sort the yong prince Hamblet behaved himselfe, to escape the tyranny of his uncle.

CHAPTER II

How Hamblet counterfeited the mad man, to escape the tyrannie of his uncle, and how he was tempted by a woman (through his uncles procurement) who thereby thought to undermine the Prince, and by that meanes to finde out whether he counterfeited madnesse or not: and how Hamblet would by no means bee brought to consent unto her, and what followed.

GERUTH having (as I sayd before) so much forgotten herself, the prince Hamblet perceiving himself to bee in danger of his life, as beeing abandoned of his owne mother, and forsaken of all men, and assuring himselfe that Fengon would not detract the time to send him the same way his father Horvendile was gone, to beguile the tyrant in his subtilties (that esteemed him to bee of such a minde that if he once attained to mans estate he wold not long delay the time to revenge the death of his father) counterfeiting the mad man with such craft and subtill practises, that hee made shewe as if hee had utterly lost his wittes: and under that vayle hee covered his pretence, and defended his life from the treasons and practises of the tyrant his uncle. And all though hee had beene at the schoole of the Romane Prince, who, because hee counterfeited himselfe to bee a foole, was called Brutus, yet hee imitated his fashions, and his wisedom. For every day beeing in the queenes palace, (who as then was more carefull to please her whoremaster, then ready to revenge the cruell death of her husband, or to restore her sonne to his inheritance), hee rent and tore his clothes, wallowing and lying in the durt and mire, his face all filthy and blacke, running through the streets like a man distraught, not speaking one worde, but such as seemed to proceede of madnesse and meere frenzie; all his actions and jestures beeing no other than the right countenances of a man wholly deprived of all reason and understanding, in such sort, that as then hee seemed fitte for nothing but to make sport to the pages and ruffling courtiers that attended in the court of his uncle and father-in-law. But the yong prince noted them well enough, minding one day to bee revenged in such manner, that the memorie thereof should remaine perpetually to the world.

Beholde, I pray you, a great point of a wise and brave spirite in a yong prince, by so great a shewe of imperfection in his person for advancement, and his owne imbasing and despising, to worke the meanes and to prepare the way for himselfe to bee one of the happiest kings in his age. In like sort, never any man was reputed by any of his actions more wise and prudent then Brutus, dissembling a great alteration in his minde, for that the occasion of such his devise of foolishnesse proceeded onely of a good and mature counsell and deliberation, not onely to preserve his goods, and shunne the rage of the proude tyrant, but also to open a large way to procure the baishment and utter ruine of wicked Tarquinius, and to infranchise the people (which were before oppressed) from the yoake of a great and miserable servitude. And so, not onely Brutus, but this man and worthy prince, to whom wee may also adde king David, that counterfeited the madde man among the petie kings of Palestina to preserve his life from the subtill practises of those kings. I shew this example unto such, as beeing offended with any great personage, have not sufficient means to prevaile in their intents, or revenge the injurie by them receaved. But when I speak of revenging any injury received upon a great personage or superior, it must be understood by such an one as is not our soveraigne, againste whom wee maie by no meanes resiste, nor once practise anie treason nor conspiracie against his life: and hee that will followe this course must speake and do all things whatsoever that are pleasing and acceptable to him whom hee meaneth to deceive, practise his actions, and esteeme him above all men, cleane contrarye to his owne intent and meaning; for that is rightly to playe and counterfeite the foole, when a man is constrained to dissemble and kisse his hand, whome in hearte hee could wishe an hundred foote depth under the earth, so hee mighte never see him more, if this were not a thing wholly to bee disliked in a christian, who by no meanes ought to have a bitter gall, or desires infected with revenge. Hamblet, in this sorte counterfeiting the madde man, many times did divers actions of great and deepe consideration, and often made such and so fitte answeres, that a wise man would soone have judged from what spirite so fine an invention mighte proceede; for that standing by the fire and sharpning sticks like poynards and prickes, one in smiling manner asked him wherefore he made those little staves so sharpe at the points? I prepare (saith he) piersing dartes and sharpe arrowes to revenge my fathers death. Fooles, as I said before, esteemed those his words as nothing; but men of quicke spirits, and such as hadde a deeper reache began to suspect somewhat, esteeming that under that kinde of folly there lay hidden a greate and rare subtilty, such as one day might bee prejudiciall to their prince, saying, that under colour of such rudenes he shadowed a crafty pollicy, and by his devised simplicitye, he concealed a sharp and pregnant spirit: for which cause they counselled the king to try and know, if it were possible, how to discover the intent and meaning of the yong prince; and they could find no better nor more fit invention to intrap him, then to set some faire and beawtifull woman in a secret place, that with flattering speeches and all the craftiest meanes she could use, should purposely seek to allure his mind to have his pleasure of her: for the nature of all young men, (especially such as are brought up wantonlie) is so transported with the desires of the flesh, and entreth so greedily into the pleasures therof, that it is almost impossible to cover the foul affection, neither yet to dissemble or hyde the same by art or industry, much lesse to shunne it. What cunning or subtilty so ever they use to cloak theire pretence, seeing occasion offered, and that in secret, especially in the most inticing sinne that rayneth in man, they cannot chuse (being constrayned by voluptuousnesse) but fall to naturall effect and working. To this end certaine courtiers were appointed to leade Hamblet into a solitary place within the woods, whether they brought the woman, inciting him to take their pleasures together, and to imbrace one another, but the subtill practices used in these our daies, not to try if men of great account bee extract out of their wits, but rather to deprive them of their strength, vertue and wisedome, by meanes of such devilish practitioners, and intefernall spirits, their domestical servants, and ministers of corruption. And surely the poore prince at this assault had him in great danger, if a gentlman (that in Horvendiles time had been nourished with him) had not showne himselfe more affectioned to the bringing up he had received with Hamblet, then desirous to please the tirant, who by all meanes sought to intangle the sonne in the same nets wherein the father had ended his dayes. This gentleman bare the courtyers (appointed as aforesaide of this treason) company, more desiring to give the prince instruction what he should do, then to intrap him, making full account that the least showe of perfect sence and wisedome that Hamblet should make would be sufficient to cause him to loose his life: and therefore by certain signes, he gave Hamblet intelligence in what danger hee was like to fall, if by any meanes hee seemed to obaye, or once like the wanton toyes and vicious provocations of the gentlewoman sent thither by his uncle. Which much abashed the prince, as then wholy beeing in affection to the lady, but by her he was likewise informed of the treason, as being one that from her infancy loved and favored him, and would have been exceeding sorrowfull for his misfortune, and much more to leave his companie without injoying the pleasure of his body, whome shee loved more than herselfe. The prince in this sort having both deceived the courtiers, and the ladyes expectation, that affirmed and swore that hee never once offered to have his pleasure of the woman, although in subtilty hee affirmed the contrary, every man there upon assured themselves that without all doubt he was distraught of his sences, that his braynes were as then wholly void of force, and incapable of reasonable apprehension, so that as then Fengons practise took no effect: but for al that he left not off, still seeking by al meanes to finde out Hambet's subtilty, as in the next chapter you shall perceive.

CHAPTER III

How Fengon, uncle to Hamblet, a second time to intrap him in his politick madnes, caused one of his counsellors to be secretly hidden in the queens chamber, behind the arras, to heare what speeches passed between Hamblet and the Queen; and how Hamblet killed him, and escaped that danger, and what followed.

AMONG the friends of Fengon, there was one that above al the rest doubted of Hamblets practises in counterfeiting the madman, who for that cause said, that it was impossible that so craftie a gallant as Hamblet, that counterfeited the foole, should be discovered with so common and unskilfull practises, which might easily bee perceived, and that to finde out his politique pretence it were necessary to invent some subtill and crafty meanes, more attractive, whereby the gallant might not have the leysure to use his accustomed dissimulation; which to effect he said he knew a fit waie, and a most convenient meane to effect the kings desire, and thereby to intrap Hamblet in his subtilties, and cause him of his owne accord to fall into the net prepared for him, and thereby evidently shewe his secret meaning. His devise was thus, that King Fengon should make as though he were to goe some long voyage concerning affaires of great importance, and that in the meane time Hamblet should be shut up alone in a chamber with his mother, wherein some other should secretly be hidden behind the hangings, unknowne either to him or his mother, there to stand and heere their speeches, and the complots by them to bee taken concerning the accomplishment of the dissembling fooles pretence; assuring the king that if there were any point of wisedome and perfect sence in the gallants spirit, that without all doubte he would easily discover it to his mother, as being devoid of all feare that she would utter or make knowne his secret intent, beeing the woman that had borne him in her bodie, and nourished him so carefully; and withall offered himselfe to be the man that should stand and harken and beare witnesse of Hamblets speeches with his mother, that hee might not be esteemed a counsellor in such a case wherein he refused to be the executioner for the behoofe and service of his prince. This invention pleased the king exceeding well, esteeming it as the onelie and soveraigne remedie to heale the prince of his lunacie; and to that ende making a long voyage, issued out of his pallace, and road to hunt in the forrest. Meane time the counsellor entred secretly into the queenes chamber, and there hid himselfe behind the arras, not long before the queene and Hamblet came thither, who beeing craftie and pollitique, as soone as hee was within the chamber, doubting some treason, and fearing if he should speake severely and wisely to his mother touching his secret practises he should be understood, and by that meanes intercepted, used his ordinary manner of dissimulation, and began to come like a cocke beating with his armes, (in such manner as cockes use to strike with their wings) upon the hangings of the chamber: whereby, feeling something stirring under them, he cried, A rat, a rat! and presently drawing his sworde thrust it into the hangings, which done, pulled the counsellour (halfe dead) out by the heeles, made an end of killing him, and beeing slaine, cut his bodie in pieces, which he caused to be boyled, and then cast it into an open vaulte or privie, that so it mighte serve for foode to the hogges. By which meanes having discovered the ambushe, and given the inventer thereof his just rewarde, hee came againe to his mother, who in the meane time wepte and tormented her selfe to see all her hopes frustrate, for that what fault soever she had committed, yet was shee sore grieved to see her onely child made a mere mockery, every man reproaching her with his folly, one point whereof she had as then seene before her eyes, which was no small pricke to her conscience, esteeming that the gods sent her that punishment for joyning incestuously in marriage with the tyrannous murtherer of her husband, who like wise ceased not to invent all the meanes he could to bring his nephew to his ende, accusing his owne naturall indiscretion, as beeing the ordinary guide of those that so much desire the pleasures of the bodie, who shutting up the waie to all reason, respect not what maie ensue of their lightnes and great inconstancy, and how a pleasure of small moment is sufficient to give them cause of repentance during their lives, and make them curse the daye and time that ever any such apprehensions entred into theire mindes, or that they closed their eies to reject the honestie requisite in ladies of her qualitie, and to despise the holy institution of those dames that had gone before her, both in nobilitie and vertue, calling to mind the great prayses and commendations given by the danes to Rinde, daughter to king Rothere, the chastest lady in her time, and withall so shamefast that she would never consent to marriage with any prince or knight whatsoever; surpassing in vertue all the ladyes of her time, as shee herselfe surmounted them in beawtie, good behaviour, and comelines. And while in this sort she sate tormenting herselfe, Hamlet entred into the chamber, who having once againe searched every corner of the same, distrusting his mother as well as the rest, and perceiving himselfe to bee alone, began in sober and discreet manner to speak unto her, saying,

What treason is this, O most infamous woman! of all that ever prostrated themselves to the will of an abhominable whore monger, who, under the vail of a dissembling creature, covereth the most wicked and detestable crime that man could ever imagine, or was committed. Now may I be assured to trust you, that like a vile wanton adultresse, altogether impudent and given over to her pleasure, runnes spreading forth her armes joyfully to imbrace the trayterous villanous tyrant that murthered my father, and most incestuously receivest the villain into the lawfull bed of your loyall spouse, imprudently entertaining him in steede of the deare father of your miserable and discomforted soone, if the gods grant him not the grace speedilie to escape from a captivity so unworthie the degree he holdeth, and the race and noble familie of his ancestors. Is this the part of a queene, and daughter to a king? to live like a brute beast (and like a mare that yieldeth her bodie to the horse that hath beaten hir companion awaye), to followe the pleasure of an abhominable king that hath murthered a farre more honester and better man then himself in massacring Horvendile, the honor and glory of the Danes, who are now esteemed of no force nor valour at all, since the shining splendure of knighthood was brought to an end by the most wickedest and cruellest villaine living upon earth. I, for my part, will never account him for my kinsman, nor once knowe

him for mine uncle, nor you my deer mother, for not having respect to the blud that ought to have united us so
straightly together, and who neither with your honor nor
without suspicion of consent to the death of your husband
could ever have agreed to have marryed with his cruell
enemie. O, queene Geruthe, it is the part of a bitch to
couple with many, and desire acquaintance of divers mas-
tiffes: it is licentiousnes only that hath made you deface
out of your minde the memory of the valor and vertues
of the good king your husband and my father: it was an
unbrideled desire that guided the daughter of Roderick
to imbrace the tyrant Fengon, and not to remember Horvendile (unworthy of so strange intertainment), neither
that he killed his brother traiterously, and that shee being his fathers wife betrayed him, although he so well favoured and loved her, that for her sake he utterly bereaved
Norway of her riches and valiant souldiers to augment
the treasures of Roderick, and make Geruthe wife to the
hardyest prince in Europe: it is not the parte of a woman,
much lesse of a princesse, in whome all modesty, curtesse,
compassion, and love ought to abound, thus to leave her
deare child to fortune in the bloody and murtherous hands
of a villain and traytor. Bruite beasts do not so, for lyons,
tygers, ounces and leopards fight for the safety and defence of their whelpes; and birds that have beakes, claws,
and wings, resist such as would ravish them of their yong
ones; but you, to the contrary, expose and deliver mee to
death, whereas ye should defend me. Is not this as much
as if you should betray me, when you knowing the per-

versenes of the tyrant and his intents, ful of deadly counsell as touching the race and image of his brother, have
not once sought, nor desired to finde the meanes to save
your child (and only son) by sending him into Swethland,
Norway, or England, rather than to leave him as a pray to
youre infamous adulterer? bee not offended, I praye you,
Madame, if transported with dolour and griefe, I speake
so boldely unto you, and that I respect you lesse then du-
etie requireth; for you, having forgotten mee, and wholy
rejected the memorye of the deceased K. my father, must
not bee abashed if I also surpasse the bounds and limits of
due consideration. Beholde into what distresse I am now
fallen, and to what mischiefe my fortune, and your over
great lightnesse, and want of wisdome have induced mee,
that I am constrained to playe the madde man to save my
life, in steed of using and practising armes, following ad-
ventures, and seeking all meanes to make my selfe knowne
to bee the true and undoubted heire of the valiant and
vertuous king Horvendile. It was not without cause, and
juste occasion, that my gestures, countenances, and words,
seeme all to proceed from a madman, and that I desire to
have all men esteeme mee wholly deprived of sence and
reasonable understanding, bycause I am well assured, that
he that hath made no conscience to kill his owne brother,
(accustomed to murthers, and allured with desire of gover-
nement without controll in his treasons), will not spare, to
save himselfe with the like crueltie, in the blood and flesh
of the loyns of his brother by him massacred: and, therefore, it is better for me to fayne madnesse, then to use my

right sences as nature hath bestowed them upon me; the bright shining clearnes therof I am forced to hide under this shadow of dissimulation, as the sun doth hir beams under some great cloud, when the wether in sommer time overcasteth. The face of a mad man serveth to cover my gallant countenance, and the gestures of a fool are fit for me, to the end that guiding my self wisely therein, I may preserve my life for the Danes, and the memory of my late deceased father; for the desire of revenging his death is so engraven in my heart, that if I dye not shortly, I hope to take such and so great vengeance, that these countryes shall for ever speake thereof. Neverthelesse, I must stay the time, meanes, and occasion, lest by making over great hast, I be now the cause of mine owne sodaine ruine and overthrow, and by that meanes end before I beginne to effect my hearts desire. Hee that hath to doe with a wicked, disloyall, cruell, and discourteous man must use craft and politike inventions, such as a fine witte can best imagine, not to discover his interprise; for seeing that by force I cannot effect my desire, reason alloweth me by dissimulation, subtiltie, and secret practises to prodeed therein. To conclude, weepe not (madame) to see my folly, but rather sigh and lament your owne offence, tormenting your conscience in regard of the infamie that hath so defiled the ancient renowne and glorie that (in times past) honoured queene Geruth; for wee are not to sorrowe and grieve at other mens vices, but for our owne misdeedes, and great folloyes. Desiring you, for the surplus of my proceedings, above all things (as you love your owne life and welfare) that neither the king nor any other may by any meanes know mine intent; and let me alone with the rest, for I hope in the ende to bring my purpose to effect.

Although the queene perceived herselfe neerly touched, and that Hamlet mooved her to the quicke, where she felt herself interested, neverthelesse shee forgot all disdaine and wrath, which thereby she might as then have had, hearing her selfe so sharply chiden and reprooved, for the joy she then conceaved, to behold the gallant spirit of her sonne, and to thinke what she might hope, and the easier expect of his so great policie and wisdome. But on the one side she durst not lift up her eyes to beholde him, remembering her offence, and on the other side she would gladly have imbraced her son, in regard of the wise admonitions by him given unto her, which as then quenched the flames of unbridled desire that before had moved her to affect K. Fengon, to ingraff in her heart the vertuous actions of her lawfull spouse, whom inwardly she much lamented, when she beheld the lively image and portraiture of his vertue and great wisedome in her childe, representing his fathers haughtie and valiant heart: and so, overcome and vanquished with this honest passion, and weeping most bitterly, having long time fixed her eyes upon Hamlet, as beeing ravished into some great and deepe contemplation, and as it were wholy amazed, at the last imbracing him in her armes (with the like love that a vertuous mother may or can use to kisse and entertaine her owne childe), shee spake unto him in this manner.

I know well (my sonne) that I have done thee great

wrong in marrying with Fengon, the cruell tyrant and murtherer of thy father, and my loyall spouse: but when thou shalt consider the small meanes of resistance, and the treason of the palace, with the little cause of confidence we are to expect or hope for of the courtiers, all wrought to his will, as also the power hee made ready, if I should have refused to like of him, thou wouldest rather excuse then accuse me of lasciviousnes or inconstancy, much lesse offer me that wrong to suspect that ever thy mother Geruthe once consented to the death and murther of her husband: swearing unto thee (by majestie of the Gods) that if it had layne in my power to have resisted the tyrant, although it had beene with the losse of my blood, yea and my life, I would surely have saved the life of my lord and husband, with as good a will and desire as, since that time, I have often beene a meanes to hinder and impeach the short-ning of thy life, which being taken away, I will no longer live here upon earth. For seeing that thy sences are whole and sound, I am in hope to see an easie meanes invent-ed for the revenging of thy fathers death. Neverthelesse, mine owne sweet soone, if thou hast pittie of thy selfe, or care of the memorie of thy father (although thou wilt do nothing for her that deserveth not the name of a mother in this respect), I pray thee, carie thine affayres wisely: bee not hastie, nor over furious in thy interprises, neither yet advance thy selfe more then reason shall moove thee to effect thy purpose. Thou seest there is not almost any man wherein thou mayest put thy trust, nor any woman to whom I dare utter the least part of my secrets, that would

not presently report it to thine adversarie, who, although
in outward shew he dissembleth to love thee, the better
to injoy his pleasures of me, yet he distrusteth and feareth
mee for thy sake, and is not so simple to be easily per-
swaded that thou art a foole or mad; so that if thou chance
to doe any thing that seemeth to proceed of wisedom or
policie (how secretly soever it be done) he will presently be
informed thereof, and I am greatly afraide that the devils
have shewed him what hath past at this present between
us, (fortune so much pursueth and contrarieth our ease
and welfare) or that this murther that now thou has committed be not the cause of both our destructions, which
I by no meanes will seeme to know, but will keepe secret
both thy wisedome and hardy interprise; beseeching the
Gods (my good soone) that they, guiding thy heart, directing thy counsels, and prospering thy interprise, I may see
thee possesse and injoy that which is thy right, and weare
the crowne of Denmarke, by the tyrant taken from thee;
that I may rejoyce in thy prosperitie, and therewith content my self, seeing with what courage and boldnesse thou
shalt take vengeance upon the murtherer of thy father, as
also upon all those that have assisted and favoured him
in his mutherous and bloody enterprise. Madame (sayd
Hamlet) I will put my trust in you, and from henceforth
meane not to meddle further with your affayres, beseeching you (as you love your owne flesh and blood) that you
will from hence foorth no more esteeme of the adulterer,
mine enemie whom I wil surely kill, or cause to be put
to death, in despite of all the devils in hel: and have he

never so manie flattering courtezans to defend him, yet will I bring him to his death, and they themselves also shall beare him company therein, as they have bin his perverse counsellors in the action of killing my father, and his companions in his treason, massacre and cruell enterprise. And reason requireth that, even as trayterously they then caused their prince to bee put to death, that with the like (nay well, much more) justice they should pay the interest of their fellonious actions.

You know (Madame) how Hother your grandfather, and father to the good king Roderick, having vanquished Guimon, caused him to be burnt, for that the cruell vilain had done the like to his lord Gevare, whom he betrayed in the night time. And who knoweth not that traytors and perjured persons deserve no faith nor loyaltie to be observed towardes them, and that conditions made with murtherers ought to bee esteemed as cobwebs, and accounted as if they were things never promised nor agreed upon: but if I lay handes upon Fengon, it will neither be fellonie nor treason, hee being neither my king nor my lord, but I shall justly punish him as my subject, that hath disloyaly behaved himselfe against his lord and soveraigne prince. And seeing that glory is the rewarde of the vertuous, and the honour and praise of those that do service to their naturall prince, why should not blame and dishonour accompany traytors, and ignominious death al those that dare be so bold as to lay violent hands upon sacred kings, that are friends and companions of the gods, as representing ther majestie and persons. To conclude, glorie is the

crown of vertue, and the price of constancie; and seeing
that it never accompanieth with infelicitie, but shunneth
cowardize and spirits of base and trayterous conditions,
it must necessarily followe, that either a glorious death
will be mine ende, or with my sword in hand, (laden with
tryumph and victorie) I shall bereave them of their lives
that made mine unfortunate, and darkened the beames of
that vertue which I possessed from the blood and famous
memory of my predecessors. For why should men desire
to live, when shame and infamie are the executioners that
torment their consciences, and villany is the cause that
withholdeth the heart from valiant interprises, and diver-
teth the minde from honest desire of glorie and commen-
dation, which indureth for ever? I know it is foolishly
done to gather fruit before it is ripe, and to seeke to enjoy
a benefit, not knowing whither it belong to us of right; but
I hope to effect it so well, and have so great confidence in
my fortune (that hitherto hath guided the action of my
life) that I shall not dye without revenging my selfe upon
mine enemie, and that himselfe shall be the instrument
of his owne decay, and to execute that which of my selfe I
durst not have enterprised.

After this, Fengon (as if hee had beene out some long
journey) came to the court againe, and asked for him that
had received the charge to play the intelligencer, to entrap
Hamlet in his dissembled wisedome, was abashed to heare
neither newes nor tydings of him, and for that cause asked
Hamlet what was become of him, naming the man. The
prince that never used lying, and who in all the answers

that ever he made (during his counterfeit madnesse) never strayed from the trueth (as a generous minde is a mortal enemie to untruth) answered and sayd, that the counsellor he sought for was gone downe through the privie, where being choaked by the filthynesse of the place, the hogs meeting him had filled their bellyes.

CHAPTER IIII

How Fengon the third time devised to send Hamblet to the king of England, with secret letters to have him put to death: and how Hamblet, when his companions slept, read the letters, and instead of them counterfeited others, willing the king of England to put the two messengers to death, and to marry his daughter to Hamblet, which was effected; and how Hamblet escaped out of England.

A MAN would have judged any thing, rather then that Hamblet had committed that murther, nevertheless Fengon could not content himselfe, but still his minde gave him that the foole would play him some tricke of liegerdemaine, and willingly would have killed him, but he feared king Rodericke, his grandfather, and further durst not offend the queene, mother to the foole whom she loved and much cherished, shewing great griefe and heavinesse to see him so transported out of his wits. And in that conceit, seeking to bee rid of him, determined to finde the meanes to doe it by the ayde of a stranger, making the king of England minister of his massacreing resolution, choosing rather that his friende should defile his renowne with so great a wickednesse, then himselfe to fall into perpetuall infamie by an exploit of so great crueltie, to whom hee purposed to send him, and by letters desire him to put him to death.

Hamblet, understanding that he should be sent into England, presently doubted the occasion of his voyage, and for that cause speaking to the queene, desired her not to make any shew of sorrow or griefe for his departure, but rather counterfeit a gladnesse, as being rid of his presence; whom, although she loved, yet she dayly grieved to see him in so pittifull estate, deprived of all sence and reason: desiring her further, that she should hang the hall with tapestrie, and make it fast with nayles upon the walles, and keepe the brands for him which hee had sharpened at the points, then, when as he said he made arrowes to revenge the death of his father: lastly, he counselled her, that the yeere after his departure being accomplished, she should celebrate his funerals; assuring her that at the same instant she should see him returne with great content-ment and pleasure unto her for that his voyage. Now, to beare him company were assigned two of Fengons faithfull ministers, bearing letters ingraved in wood, that contained Hamlets death, in such sort as he had advertised the king of England. But the subtile Danish prince (beeing at sea) whilst his companions slept, having read the letters, and knowne his uncles great treason, with the wicked and vil-lainous mindes of the two courtyers that led him to the slaughter, raced out the letters that concerned his death, and in stead thereof graved others, with commission to the king of England to hang his two companions; and not content to turne the death they had devised against him upon their owne neckes, wrote further, that king Fengon willed him to give his daughter to Hamlet in marriage. And so arriving in England, the messengers presented themselves to the king, giving him Fengons letters; who having read the contents, sayd nothing as then, but stayed convenient time to effect Fengons desire, meane time using the Danes familiarly, doing them that honour to sit as his table (for that kings as then were not so curiously, nor solemnely served as in these our dayes,) for in these dayes meane kings, and lords of small revenewe are as difficult and hard to bee seene, as in times past the monarches of Persia used to bee: or as it is reported of the great king of Aethyopia, who will not permit any man to see his face, which ordinarily hee covereth with a vaile. And as the messengers sate at the table with the king, subtile Hamlet was so far from being merry with them, that he would not taste one bit of meate, bread, nor cup of beare whatsoever, as then set upon the table, not without great wondering of the company, abashed to see a yong man and a stranger not to esteeme of the delicate meates and pleasant drinkes served at the banquet, rejecting them as things filthy, evill of tast, and worse prepared. The king, who for that time dissembled what he thought, caused his ghests to be conveyed into their chamber, willing one of his secret servantes to hide himselfe therein, and so to certifie him what speeches past among the Danes at their going to bed.

Now they were no sooner entred into the chamber, and those that were appointed to attend upon them gone out, but Hamlets companions asked him, why he refused to eate and drinke of that which hee found upon the table, not honouring the banquet of so great a king, that entertained them in friendly sort, with such honour and courtesie as it deserved? saying further, that hee did not well, but dishonoured him that sent him, as if he sent men into England that feared to bee poysoned by so great a king. The prince, that had done nothing without reason and prudent consideration, answered them, and sayd: What, think you, that I wil eat bread dipt in humane blood, and defile my throate with the rust of yron, and use that meat that stinketh and savoureth of mans flesh, already putrified and corrupted, and that senteth like the savour of a dead carryon, long since cast into a valt? and how woulde you have mee to respect the king, that hath the countenance of a slave; and the queene, who in stead of great majestie, hath done three things more like a woman of base parentage, and fitter for a waiting gentlewoman then beseeming a lady of her qualitie and estate. And having sayd so, used many injurious and sharpe speeches as well against the king and queene, as others that had assisted at that banquet for the intertainment of the Danish ambassadors; and therein Hamblet said trueth, as hereafter you shall heare, for that in those dayes, the north parts of the worlde, living as then under Sathans lawes, were full of inchanters, so that there was not any yong gentleman whatsoever that knew not something therein sufficient to serve his turne, if need required: as yet in those dayes in Gothland and Biarmy, there are many that knew not what the Christian religion permitteth, as by reading the histories of Norway and Gothland, you maie easilie perceeve: and so Hamlet, while his father lived, had bin instructed in that devilish art, whereby the wicked spirite abuseth mankind, and advertiseth him (as he can) of things past.

It toucheth not the matter herein to discover the parts of devination in man, and whether this prince, by reason of his over great melancholy, had received those impressions, devining that, which never any but himselfe had before declared, like the philosophers, who discoursing of divers deep points of philosophie, attribute the force of those divinations to such as are saturnists by complection, who oftentimes speake of things which, their fury ceasing, they then alreadye can hardly understand who are the pronouncers; and for that cause Plato saith, many deviners and many poets, after the force and vigour of their fier beginneth to lessen, do hardly understand what they have written, although intreating of such things, while the spirite of devination continueth upon them, they doe in such sorte discourse thereof that the authors and inventers of the arts themselves by them alledged, commend their discourses and subtill disputations. Likewise I mean not to relate that which divers men beleeve, that a reasonable soul becometh the habitation of a meaner sort of devels, by whom men learn the secrets of things natural; and much lesse do I account of the supposed governors of the world fained by magitians, by whose means they brag to effect mervailous things. It would seeme miraculous that Hamlet shold divine in that sort, which after prooved so true (if as I said before) the devel had not knowledg of things past, but to grant it he knoweth things to come I hope you shall never finde me in so grose an error. You will compare and make equall derivation, and conjecture with those that are made by the spirit of God, and pronounced by the holy prophets, that tasted of that marvelous science, to whome onely was declared the secrets and wondrous workes of the Almighty. Yet there are some imposturious companions that impute so much devinitie to the devell, the father of lyes, that they attribute unto him the truth of the knowledge of thinges that shall happen unto men, alledging the conference of Saul with the witch, although one example out of the Holy Scriptures, specially set downe for the condemnation of wicked man, is not of force to give sufficient law to all the world; for they themselves confesse that they can devine, not according to the universal cause of things, but by signes borrowed from such like causes, which are all waies alike, and by those conjectures they can give judgement of the thinges to come, but all this beeing grounded upon a weake support, (which is a simple conjecture) and having so slender a foundation, as some foolish or late experience the fictions being voluntarie. It should be a great folly in a man of good judgment, specially one that imbraceth the preaching of the gospell, and seeketh after no other but the trueth thereof, to repose upon any of these likelihoods or writings full of deceipt.

As touching magical operations, I will grant them somewhat therein, finding divers histories that write thereof, and that the Bible maketh mention, and forbiddeth the use thereof: yea, the lawes of the gentiles and ordinances of emperors have bin made against it in such sort, that Mahomet, the great hereticke and friend of the devell, by whose subtiltyes hee abused most part of the east countries, hath ordained great punishments for such as use and practise those unlawfull and damnable arts, which, for this time leaving of, let us returne to Hamblet, brought up in these abuses, according to the manner of his country, whose companions hearing his answere reproached him of folly, saying that hee could by no meanes show a greater point of indiscretion, then in despising that which is lawfull, and rejecting that which all men receaved as a necessary thing, and that hee had not grossely so forgotten himselfe as in that sort to accuse such and so excellent a man as the king of England, and to slander the queene, being then as famous and wise a princes as any at that day raigning in the ilands thereabouts, to cause him to be punished according to his deserts; but he, continuing in his dissimulation, mocked him, saying that hee had not done any thing that was not good and most true. On the other side, the king being advertised thereof by him that stood to heare the discourse, judged presently that Hamlet, speaking so ambiguously, was either a perfect foole, or else one of the wisest princes in his time, answering so sodainly, and so much to the purpose upon the demaund by his companions made touching his behaviour; and the better to find the trueth, caused the babler to be sent for, of whome inquiring in what place the corne grew whereof he made bread for his table, and whether in that ground there were not some signes or newes of a battaile fought, whereby humaine blood had therein been shed? the babler answered that not far from thence there lay a field ful of dead mens bones, in times past slaine in a battaile, as by the greate heapes of wounded sculles mighte well appeare, and for that the ground in that parte was become fertiler then other grounds, by reason of the fatte and humours of the dead bodies, that every yeer the farmers used there to have in the best wheat they could finde to serve his majesties house. The king perceiving it to be true, according to the yong princes wordes, asked where the hogs had bin fed that were killed to be served at his table? and answere was made him, that those hogs getting out of the said fielde wherein they were kepte, had found the bodie of a thiefe that had beene hanged for his demerits, and had eaten thereof: whereat the king of England being abashed, would needs know with what water the beer he used to drinke of had beene brued? which having knowne, he caused the river to bee digged somewhat deeper, and therin found great store of swords and rustie armours, that gave an ill savour to the drinke. It were good I should heere dilate somewhat of Merlins prophesies, which are said to be spoken of him before he was fully one yeere old; but if you consider wel what hath al reddy been spoken, it is no hard matter to divine of things past, although the minister of Sathan therein played his part, giving sodaine and prompt answeres to this yong prince, for that herein are nothing but natural things, such as were wel known to be true, and therefore not needfull to dreame of thinges to come. This knowne, the king, greatly moved with a certaine curiostie to knowe why the Danish prince saide that he had the countenance of a slave, suspecting thereby that he reproached the basenes of his blood, and that he wold affirme that never any prince had bin his sire, wherein to satisfie himselfe he went to his mother, and leading her into a secret chamber, which he shut as soone as they were entred, desired her of her honour to shewe him of whome he was ingendred in this world. The good lady, wel assured that never any man had bin acquainted with her love touching any other man then her husband, sware that the king her husband onely was the man that had enjoyed the pleasures of her body; but the king her sonne, alreadie with the truth of the Danish princes answers, threatned his mother to make her tell by force, if otherwise she would not confesse it, who for feare of death acknowledged that she had prostrated her body to a slave, and made him father to the king of England; whereat the king was abashed, and wholy ashamed. I give them leave to judge who esteeming themselves honester than theire neighbours, and supposing that there can be nothing amisse in their houses, make more enquirie then is requisite to know the which they would rather not have known. Neverthelesse dissembling what he thought, and biting upon the bridle, rather then he would deprive himselfe by publishing the lasciviousnes

of his mother, thought better to leave a great sin unpunished, then thereby to make himselfe contemptible to his
subjects, who peradventure would have rejected him, as
not desiring to have a bastard to raigne over so great a
kingdome.

But as he was sorry to hear his mothers confession, on
the other side he tooke great pleasure in the subtilty and
quick spirit of the yong prince, and for that cause went
unto him to aske him, why he had reproved three things
in his queene convenient for a slave, and savouring more
of basenes then of royaltie, and far unfit for the majesty of
a great prince? The king, not content to have received a
great displeasure by knowing him selfe to be a bastard, and
to have heard with what injuries he charged her whom hee
loved best in all the world, would not content himself untill he also understood that which displeased him, as much
as his owne proper disgrace, which was that his queen
was the daughter of a chambermaid, and with all noted
certaine foolish countenances she made, which not onely
shewed of what parentage she came, but also that hir hu-
mors savored of the basenes and low degree of hir parents,
whose mother, he assured the king, was as then yet holden
in servitude. The king admiring the young prince, and be-
houlding in him some matter of greater respect then in
the common sort of men, gave him his daughter in marriage, according to the counterfet letters by him devised,
and the next day caused the two servants of Fengon to be
executed, to satisfie, as he thought, the king's desire. But
Hamlet, although the sport plesed him wel, and that the

king of England could not have done him a greater favour, made as though he had been much offended, threatning the king to be revenged, but the king, to appease him, gave him a great sum of gold, which Hamlet caused to be molten, and put into two staves, made hollow for the same purpose, to serve his tourne there with as neede should require; for of all other the kings treasures he took nothing with him into Denmark but onely those two staves, and as soone as the yeere began to bee at an end, having somewhat before obtained licence of the king his father in law to depart, went for Denmarke; then, with all the speed hee could to returne againe into England to marry his daughter, and so set sayle for Denmarke.

CHAPTER V

How Hamblet, having escaped out of England, arrived in Denmarke the same day that the Danes were celebrating his funerals, supposing him to be dead in England; and how he revenged his fathers death upon his uncle and the rest of the courtiers; and what followed.

HAMBLET in that sort sayling into Denmark, being arrived in the contry, entered into the pallace of his uncle the same day that they were celebrating his funeralls, and going into the hall, procured no small astonishment and wonder to them all, no man thinking other but that hee had beene deade: among the which many of them rejoyced not a little for the pleasure which they knew Fengon would conceave for so pleasant a losse, and some were sadde, as remembering the honourable king Horvendile, whose victories they could by no meanes forget, much lesse deface out of theire memories that which apperteined unto him, who as then greatly rejoyced to see a false report spread of Hamlets death, and that the tyrant had not as yet obtained his will of the heire of Jutie, but rather hoped God would restore him to his sences againe for the good and welfare of that province. Their amazement at the last beeing tourned into laughter, all that as then were assistant at the funerall banquet of him whome they esteemed dead, mocked each at other, for having beene so simply deceived, and wondering at the prince, that in his so long a voyage he had not recovered any of his sences, asked what was become of them that had borne him company into Greate Brittain? to whome he made answere (shewing them the two hollow staves, wherein he had put his molten golde, that the King of England had given him to appease his fury, concerning the murther of his two companions), and said, Here they are both. Whereat many that already knew his humours, presently conjectured that hee had plaide some trick of legerdemane, and to deliver himselfe out of danger, had throwne them into the pitte prepared for him: so that fearing to follow after them and light upon some evil adventure, they went presently out of the court. And it was well for them that they didde so, considering the tragedy acted by him the same daie, beeing accounted his funerall, but in trueth theire last daies, that as then rejoyced for their overthrow; for when every man busied himselfe to make good cheare, and Hamlets arivall provoked them more to drinke and carouse, the prince himselfe at that time played the butler and a gentleman attending on the tables, not suffering the pots nor goblets to bee empty, whereby hee gave the noble men such store of liquor, that all of them being ful laden with wine and gorged with meate, were constrained to lay themselves downe in the same place where they had supt, so much their sences were dulled, and overcome with the fire of over great drinking (a vice common and familiar among the Almaines, and other nations inhabiting the north parts of the world) which when Hamlet perceiving, and finding so good opportunitie to effect his purpose and bee revenged of his enemies, and by the means to abandon the actions, gestures, and apparel of a mad man, occasion so fitly finding his turn, and as it were effecting it selfe, failed not to take hold therof, and seeing those drunken bodies, filled with wine, lying like hogs upon the ground, some sleeping, others vomiting the over great abundance of wine which without measure they had swallowed up, made the hangings about the hall to fall downe and cover them all over; which he nailed to the ground, being boorded, and at the ends thereof he stuck the brands, whereof I spake before, by him sharpned, which served for prickes, binding and tying the hangings in such sort, that what force soever they used to loose themselves, it was unpossible to get from under them: and presently he set fire to the foure corners of the hal, in such sort, that all that were as then therein not one escaped away, but were forced to purge their sins by fire, and dry up the great aboundance of liquor by them received into their bodies, all of them dying in the inevitable and mercilesse flames of the whot and burning fire: which the prince perceiving, became wise, and knowing that his uncle, before the end of the banquet, had withdrawn himselfe into his chamber, which stood apart from the place where the fire burnt, went thither, and entring into the chamber, layd hand upon the sword of his fathers murtherer, leaving his own in the place, which while he was at the banket some of the courtiers had nailed fast into the scaberd, and going to Fengon said: I wonder, disloyal king, how thou canst sleep heer at thine ease, and al thy pallace is burnt, the fire thereof having burnt the greatest part of thy courtiers and ministers of thy cruelty, and detestable tirannies; and which is more, I cannot imagin how thou sholdst wel assure thy self and thy estate, as now to take thy ease, seeing Hamlet so neer thee armed with the shafts by him prepared long since, and at this present is redy to revenge the traiterous injury by thee done to his lord and father.

Fengon, as then knowing the truth of his nephews subtile practise, and hering him speak with stayed mind, and which is more, perceived a sword naked in his hand, which he already lifted up to deprive him of his life, leaped quickly out of the bed, taking holde of Hamlets sworde, that was nayled into the scaberd, which as hee sought to pull out, Hamlet gave him such a blowe upon the chine of the necke, that hee cut his head cleane from his shoulders, and as he fell to the ground sayd, This just and violent death is a just reward for such as thou art: now go thy wayes, and when thou commest in hell, see thou forget

not to tell thy brother (whom thou trayterously slewest),
that it was his sonne that sent thee thither with the message, to the ende that beeing comforted thereby, his soule
may rest among the blessed spirits, and quit mee of the
obligation that bound me to pursue his vengeance upon
mine owne blood, that seeing it was by thee that I lost
the chiefe thing that tyed me to this aliance and consanguinitie. A man (to say the trueth) hardie, courageous, and
worthy of eternall comendation, who arming himself with
a crafty, dissembling, and strange shew of beeing distract
out of his wits, under that pretence deceived the wise,
pollitike, and craftie, thereby not onely preserving his life
from the treasons and wicked practises of the tyrant, but
(which is more) by a new and unexpected kinde of punishment, revenged his fathers death, many yeeres after the
act committed: in no such sort that directing his courses
with such prudence, and effecting his purposes with so
great boldnes and constancie, he left a judgement to be
decyded among men of wisdom, which was more commendable in him, his constancy or magnanimitie, or his
wisdom in ordring his affaires, according to the premedit-
able determination he had conceaved.

If vengeance ever seemed to have any shew of justice, it is then, when pietie and affection constraineth us
to remember our fathers unjustly murdered, as the things
wherby we are dispensed withal, and which seeke the
means not to leave treason and murther unpunished: seeing David a holy and just king, and of nature simple, courteous, and debonaire, yet when he dyed he charged his

soone Salomon (that succeeded him in his throane) not to suffer certaine men that had done him injurie to escape unpunished. Not that this holy king (as then ready to dye, and to give account before God of all his actions) was carefull of desirous of revenge, but to leave this example unto us, that where the prince or countrey is interessed, the desire of revenge cannot by any meanes (how small soever) beare the title of condemnation, but is rather commendable and worthy of praise: for otherwise the good kings of Juda, nor other had not pursued them to death, that had offended their predecessors, if God himself had not inspired and ingraven that desire within their hearts. Hereof the Athenian lawes beare witnesse, whose custome was to erect images in remembrance of those men that, revenging the injuries of the commonwealth, boldly massacred tyrants and such as troubled the peace and welfare of the citizens.

Hamblet, having in this manner revenged himselfe, durst not presently declare his action to the people, but to the contrary determined to worke by policie, so to give them intelligence, what he had done, and the reason that drewe him thereunto: so that beeing accompanied with such of his fathers friends that then were rising, he stayed to see what the people would doe when they shoulde heare of that sodaine and fearefull action. The next morning the townes bordering there aboutes, desiring to know from whence the flames of fire proceeded the night before they had seene, came thither, and perceiving the kings pallace burnt to ashes, and many bodyes (most part consumed) lying among the ruines of the house, all of them were much abashed, nothing being left of the palace but the foundation. But they were much more amased to beholde the body of the king all bloody, and his head cut off lying hard by him; whereat some began to threaten revenge, yet not knowing against whom; others beholding so lamentable a spectacle, armed themselves, the rest rejoycing, yet not daring to make any shewe thereof; some detesting the crueltie, others lamenting the death of their Prince, but the greatest part calling Horvendiles murther to remembrance, acknowledging a just judgement from above, that had throwne downe the pride of the tyrant. And in this sort, the diversities of opinions among that multitude of people being many, yet every man ignorant what would be the issue of that tragedie, none stirred from thence, neither yet attempted to move any tumult, every man fearing his owne skinne, and distrusting his neighbour, esteeming each other to bee consenting to the massacre.

CHAPTER VI

How Hamlet, having slaine his Uncle, and burnt his Palace, made an Oration to the Danes to shew them what he done; and how they made him King of Denmark; and what followed.

HAMLET then seeing the people to be so quiet, and most part of them not using any words, all searching onely and simply the cause of this ruine and destruction, not minding to loose any time, but ayding himselfe with the commodotie thereof, entred among the multitude of people, and standing in the middle spake unto them as followeth.

If there be any among you (good people of Denmark) that as yet have fresh within your memories the wrong done to the valiant king Horvendile, let him not be mooved, nor thinke it strange to behold the confused, hydeous, and fearfull spectacle of this present calamitie: if there be any man that affecteth fidelitie, and alloweth of the love and dutie that man is bound to shewe his parents, and find it a just cause to call to remembrance the injuryes and wrongs that have been done to our progenitors, let him not be ashamed beholding this massacre, much lesse offended to see so fearfull a ruine both of men and of the bravest house in all this countrey: for the hand that hath done this justice could not effect it by any other meanes, neither yet was it lawfull for him to doe it otherwise, then by ruinating both sensible and unsensible things, therby to preserve the memorie of so just a vengeance.

I see well (my good friends) and am very glad to know so good attention and devotion in you, that you are sorrie (before your eyes) to see Fengon so murthered, and without a head, which heeretofore you acknowledged for your commander; but I pray you remember this body is not the body of a king, but of an execrable tyrant, and a parricide most detestable. Oh Danes! the spectacle was much more hydeous when Horvendile your king was murthered by his brother. What should I say a brother! nay, rather by the most abhominable executioner that ever beheld the same. It was you that saw Horvendiles members massacred, and that with teares and lamentations accompanied him to the grave; his body disfigured, hurt in a thousand places, and misused in ten times as many fashions. And who doubteth (seeing experience hath taught you) that the tyrant (in massacring your lawfull king) sought onely to infringe the ancient liberties of the common people? and it was one hand onely, that murthering Horvendile, cruelly dispoyled him of life, and by the same meanes unjustly bereaved you of your ancient liberties, and delighted more in oppression then to embrace the plesant countenance of prosperous libertie without adventuring for the same. And what mad man is he that delighteth more in the tyrany of Fengon then in the clemencie and renewed courtesie of Horvendile? If it bee so, that by clemencie and affabilitie the hardest and stoutest hearts are molified and made tractable, and that evill and hard usage causeth subjects to be outragious and unruly, why behold you not the debonair cariage of the first, to compare it with the cruelties and insolencies of the second, in every respect as cruell and barbarous as his brother was gentle, meeke, and courteous? Remember, O you Danes, remember what love and amitie Horvendile shewed unto you; with what equitie and justice he swayed the great affaires of this kingdome, and with what humanitie and courtisie he defended and cherished you, and then I am assured that the simplest man among you will both remember and acknowledge that he had a most peaceable, just, and righteous king taken from him, to place in his throane a tyrant and murtherer of his brother: one that hath perverted all right, abolished the auncient lawes of our fathers, contaminated the memories of our ancestors, and by his wickednesse polluted the integritie of this kingdome, upon the necke thereof having placed the troublesome yoak of heavie servitude, abolishing that libertie wherein Horvendile used to maintaine you, and suffered you to live at your ease. And should you now bee sorrie to see the ende of your mischiefes, and that this miserable wretch, pressed downe with the burthen of his offences, at this present payeth the usury of the parricide committed upon the body of his brother, and would not himselfe be the revenger of the outrage done to me, whom he sought to deprive of mine inheritance, taking from Denmark a lawfull successor, to plant a wicked stranger, and bring into captivitie those that my father had infranchised and delivered out of misery and bondage? And what man is he, that having any sparke of wisdom, would esteem a good deed to be an injury, and account pleasures equal with wrongs and evident outrages? It were then great folly and temerity in princes and valiant commanders in the wars to expose themselves to perils and hazards of their lives for the welfare of the common people, if that for a recompence they should reape hatred and indignation of the multitude. To what end should Hother have punished Balder, if, in steed of recompence, the Danes and Swethlanders had banished him to receive and accept the successors of him that desired nought but his ruine and overthrowe? What is hee that hath so small feeling of reason and equitie, that would be grieved to see treason rewarded with the like, and that an evill act is punished with just demerit in the partie himselfe that was the occasion? who was ever sorrowfull to behold the murtherer of innocents brought to his end, or what man weepeth to see a just massacre done upon a tyrant, usurper, villaine, and bloody personage?

I perceive you are attentive, and abashed for not knowing the author of your deliverance, and sorry that you cannot tell to whom you should bee thankefull for such and so great a benefit as the destruction of a tyrant, and the overthrow of the place that was the storehouse of his villanies, and the true receptacle of all the theeves and traytors in this kingdome: but beholde (here in your presence) him that brought so good an enterprise to effect. It is I (my good friends), it is I, that confesse I have taken vengeance for the violence done unto my lord and father, and for the subjection and servitude that I perceived in this countrey, whereof I am the just and lawfull successor. It is I alone, that have done this piece of worke, whereunto you ought to have lent me your handes, and therein have ayded and assisted me. I have only accomplished that which all of you might justly have effected, by good reason, without falling into any point of treason or fellonie. It is true that I hope so much of your good willes towards the deceased king Horvendile, and that the remembrances of his vertues is yet so fresh within your memories, that if I had required your aide herein, you would not have denied it,

specially to your naturall prince. But it liked mee best to
doe it my selfe alone, thinking it a good thing to punish
the wicked without hazarding the lives of my friends and
loyall subjects, not desiring to burthen other mens shoulders with this weight; for that I made account to effect it
well inough without exposing any man into danger, and
by publishing the same should cleane have overthrowne
the device, which at this present I have so happily bought
to passe. I have burnt the bodyes of the courtiers to ashes,
being companions in the mischiefs and treasons of the
tyrant; but I have left Fengon whole, that you might punish his dead carkasse (seeing that when hee lived you durst
not lay hands upon him), to accomplish the full punishment and vengeance due unto him, and so satisfie your
choller upon the bones of him that filled his greedy hands
and coffers with your riches, and shed the blood of your
brethren and friends. Bee joyfull, then (my good friends);
make ready the nosegay for this usurping king: burne his
abhominable body, boyle his lascivious members, and cast
the ashes of him that hath beene hurtfull to all the world
into the ayre: drive from you the sparkes of pitie, to the end
that neither silver, nor christall cup, nor sacred tombe may
be the restfull habitation of the reliques and bones of so
detestable a man: let not one trace of a parricide be seene,
nor your countrey defiled with the presence of the least
member of this tyrant without pity, that your neighbors
may not smell the contagion, nor our land the polluted
infection of a body condemned for his wickednes. I have
done my part to present him to you in this sort; now it be-

longs to you to make an end of the worke, and put to the last hand of dutie whereunto your severall functions call you; for in this sort you must honor abhominable princes, and such ought to be the funerall of a tyrant, parricide, and usurper, both of the bed and patrimony that no way belonged unto him, who having bereaved his countrey of liberty, it is fit that the land refuse to give him a place for the eternal rest of his bones.

O my good friends, seeing you know the wrong that hath bin done unto mee, what my griefs are, and in what misery I have lived since the death of the king, my lord and father, and seeing that you have both known and tasted these things then, when as I could not conceive the outrage that I felt, what neede I recite it unto you? what benefit would it be to discover it before them that knowing it would burst (as it were with despight) to heare of my hard chance, and curse Fortune for so much imbasing a royall prince, as to deprive him of his majesty, although not any of you durst so much as shew one sight of sorrow or sadnes? You know how my father in law conspired my death, and sought by divers meanes to take away my life; how I was forsaken of the queen my mother, mocked of my friends, and dispised of mine own subjects: hetherto I have lived laden with griefe, and wholy confounded in teares, my life still accompanied with fear and suspition, expecting the houre when the sharp sword would make an ende of my life and miserable anguishes. How many times, counterfeiting the mad man, have I heard you pitty my distresse, and secretly lament to see me disinherited?

and yet no man sought to revenge the death of my father,
nor to punish the treason of my incestuous uncle, full of
murthers and massacres. This charitie ministred comfort,
and your affectionate complaints made me evidently see
your good wills, that you had in memorie the calamity
of your prince, and within your harts ingraven the desire
of vengeance for the death of him that deserved a long
life. And what heart can bee so hard and untractable, or
spirit to severe, cruel, and rigorous, that would not relent
at the remembrance of my extremities, and take pitty of
an orphan child, so abandoned of the world? What eyes
were so voyd of moysture but would distill a field of tears,
to see a poore prince assaulted by his owne subjects, betrayed by his mother, pursued by his uncle, and so much
oppressed that his friends durst not shew the effects of
their charitie and good affection? O (my good friends)
shew pity to him whom you have nourished, and let your
harts take some compassion upon the memory of my misfortunes! I speak to you that are innocent of al treason,
and never defiled your hands, spirits, nor desires with the
blud of the greate and vertuous king Horvendile. Take
pity upon the queen, sometime your soveraign lady, and
my right honorable mother, forced by the tyrant, and rejoyce to see the end and extinguishing of the object of her
dishonor, which constrained her to be lesse pitiful to her
own blood, so far as to imbrace the murtherer of her own
dear spouse, charging her selfe with a double burthen of
infamy and incest, together with injuring and disannul-
ling of her house, and the ruine of her race. This hath bin

the occasion that made me counterfet folly, and cover my
intents under a vaile of meer madnes, which hath wisdom
and pollicy therby to inclose the fruit of this vengeance,
which, that it hath attained to the ful point of efficacy and
perfect accomplishment, you yourselves shall bee judges;
for touching this and other things concerning my profit,
and the managing of great affairs, I refer my self to your
counsels, and there unto am fully determined to yeeld, as
being those that trample under your feet the murtherers of
my father, and despise the ashes of him that hath polluted
and violated the spouse of his brother, by him massacred;
that hath committed felony against his lord, traiterously
assailed the majesty of his king, and odiously thralled his
contry under servitude and bondage, and you his loyall
subjects, from whom he, bereaving your liberty, feared
not to ad incest to parricide, detestable to al the world.
To you also it belongeth by dewty and reason commonly
to defend and protect Hamlet, the minister and executor
of just vengeance, who being jealous of your honour and
your reputation, hath hazarded himself, hoping you will
serve him for fathers, defenders, and tutors, and regarding
him in pity, restore him to his goods and inheritances. It
is I that have taken away the infamy of my contry, and
extinguished the fire that imbraced your fortunes. I have
washed the spots that defiled the reputation of the queen,
overthrowing both the tirant and the tiranny, and beguil-
ing the subtilties of the craftiest deceiver in the world, and
by that meanes brought his wickednes and impostures to
an end. I was grieved at the injurie committed both to my

father and my native country, and have slaine him that
used more rigorus commandements over you, then was
either just or convenient to be used unto men that have
commaunded that valiantest nations in the world. Seeing,
then, he was such a one to you, it is reason that you ack-
owledge the benefit, and thinke wel of for the good I had
done your posterity, and admiring my spirit and wisdome,
chuse me your king, if you think me worthy of the place.
You see I am the author of your preservation, heire of my
fathers kingdome, not straying in any point from his vertuous action, no murtherer, violent parricide, nor man that
ever offended any of you, but only the vitious. I am lawfull
successor in the kingdom, and just revenger of a crime
above al others most grievous and punishable: it is to me
that you owe the benefit of your liberty receaved, and of
the subversion of that tyranny that so much afflicted you,
that hath troden under feete the yoke of the tirant, and
overwhelmed his throne, and taken the scepter out of the
hands of him that abused a holy and just authoritie; but
it is you that are to recompence those that have well deserved, you know what is the reward of so greate desert,
and being in your hands to distribute the same, it is of you
that I demand the price of my vertue, and the recompence
of my victory.

This oration of the yong prince so mooved the harts
of the Danes, and wan the affections of the nobility, that
some wept for pity, other for joy, the see the wisedome
and gallant spirit of Hamlet; and having made an end of
their sorrow, al with one consent proclaimed him king of

Jutie and Chersonnese, at this present the proper country of Denmarke. And having celebrated his coronation,
and received the homages and fidelities of his subjects, he
went into England to fetch his wife, and rejoyced with
his father in law touching his good fortune; but it wanted
little that the king of England had not accomplished that
which Fengon with all his subtilties could never attaine.

CHAPTER VII

*How Hamlet, after his coronation, went into England;
and how the king of England secretly would have put him
to death; and how he slew the king of England, and returned againe into Denmarke with two wives; and what
followed.*

HAMLET, being in England, shewed the king what
meanes hee had wrought to recover his kingdom; but
when the king of England understood of Fengons death,
he was both abashed and confused in his minde, at that
instant feeling himselfe assailed with two great passions,
for that in times past he and Fengon having bin companions together in armes, had given each other their faith
and promises, by oath, that if either of them chanced
to bee slaine by any man whatsoever, hee that survived
(taking the quarrel upon him as his owne) should never
cease till he were revenged, or at the leaste do his endea-
vour. This promise incited the barbarous king to massacre
Hamlet, but the alliance presenting it selfe before his eies,

and beholding the one deade, although his friend, and the other alive, and husband to his daughter, made him deface his desire of revenge. But in the end, the conscience of his oath and promise obtained the upper hand, and secretly made him conclude the death of his sonne in law, which enterprise after that was cause of his own death, and overrunning of the whole country of England by the cruelty and despight conceived by the king of Denmarke. I have purposely omitted the discourse of that battaile, as not much pertinent to our matter, as also, not to trouble you with too tedious a discourse, being content to shew you the end of this wise and valiant king Hamlet, who revenging himselfe upon so many enemies, and discovering all the treasons practised against his life, in the end served for a sport to fortune, and an example to all great personages that trust overmuch to the felicities of this world, that are of small moment, and lesse continuance.

The king of England perceiving that hee could not easilie effect his desire upon the king, his son in lawe, as also not being willing to break the laws and rights of hospitality, determined to make a stranger the revenger of his injury, and so accomplish his oath made to Fengon without defiling his handes with the blood of the husband of his daughter, and polluting his house by the traiterous massacring of his friend. In reading of this history, it seemeth, Hamlet should resemble another Hercules, sent into divers places of the world by Euristheus (solicited by Juno) where he knew any dangerous adventure, thereby to overthrow and destroy him; or else Bellerophon sent to Ariobatus to put him to death; or (leaving prophane histories) an other Urias, by king David appointed to bee placed in the fore front of the battaile, and the man that should bee first slain by the barbarians. For the king of Englands wife being dead not long before (although he cared not for marrying an other woman) desired his sonne in lawe to make a voyage for him into Scotland, flattering him in such sort, that he made him beleeve that his singular wisdome caused him to preferre him to that ambassage, assuring himselfe that it were impossible that Hamlet, the subtillest and wisest prince in the worlde, should take any thing in the world in hand without effecting the same.

Now the queen of Scots beeing a maid, and of a haughty courage, despised marriage with al men, as not esteeming any worthy to be her companion, in such manner that by reason of this arrogant opinion there never came any man to desire her love but she caused him to loose his life: but the Danish kings fortune was so good, that Hermetrude (for so was the queens name) hearing that Hamlet was come thither to intreat a marriage betweene her and the king of England, forgot all her pride, and dispoiling herselfe of her sterne nature, being as then determined to make him (being the greatest prince as then living) her husband, and deprive the English princesse of her spouse, whome shee thought fit for no men but herself; and so this Amazon without love, disdaining Cupid, by her free wil submitted her haughtie mind to her concupiscence. The Dane arriving in her court, desired she to see the old king of Englands letters, and mocking

at his fond appetites, whose blood as then was half con-
gealed, cast her eies upon the yong and plesant Adonis of
the North, esteeming her selfe happy to have such a pray
fallen into her hands, wherof she made her ful account to
have the possession: and to conclude, she that never had
been overcome by the grace, courtesie, valor, or riches of
anie prince nor lord whatsoever, was as then vanquished
with the onelie report of the subtilties of the Dane; who
knowing that he was already fianced to the daughter of
the king of England, spake unto him and said: I never
looked for so great a blisse, neither from the gods nor
yet from fortune, as to behold in my countries the most
compleate prince in the North, and he that hath made
himselfe famous and renowned through all the nations
of the world, as well neighbours as strangers, for the only
respect of his vertue, wisdom, and good fortune, serving
him much in the pursuite and effect of divers thinges by
him undertaken, and thinke myselfe much beholding to
the king of England (although his malice seeketh neither
my advancement nor the good of you, my lord) to do me
so much honor as to send me so excellent a man to intre-
ate of a marriage (he being olde, and a mortal enemy to
me and mine) with mee that am such a one as every man
seeth, is not desirous to couple with a man of so base quality as he, whom you have said to be the son of a slave. But
on the other side, I marvel that the son of Horvendile,
and grand-child to king Roderick, he that by his foolish wisedom and fained madnesse surmounted the forces
and subtilties of Fengon, and obtained the kingdom of his

adversary, should so much imbase himselfe (having otherwise bin very wise and wel advised in all his actions) touching his bedfellow; and hee that for his excellency and valor surpasseth humane capacity, should stoope so lowe as to take to wife her that, issuing from a servile race, hath only the name of a king for her father, for that the basenes of her blood will alwaies cause her to shewe what are the vertues and noble qualities of her ancestors. And you, my lord, said she, are you so ignorant as not to know that mariage should not bee measured by any foolish opinion of an outward beautie, but rather by vertues, and antiquitie of race, which maketh the wife to be honored for her prudence, and never degenerating from the integritie of his ancestors: exterior beauty also is nothing, where perfection of the mind doth not accomplish and adorn that which is outwardly seen to be in the bodie, and is lost by an accident and occurrence of small moment: as also such toyes have deceived many men, and drawing them like enticing baits, have cast them headlong into the gulf of their ruine, dishonor, and utter overthrow. It was I to whom this advantage belonged, being a queen, and such a one as for nobility may compare my selfe with the greatest princes in Europe, being nothing inferiour unto any of them, neither for antiquitie of blood, nobilitie of parents, nor abundance of riches; and I am not only a queene, but such a one as that, receiving whom I will for my companion in bed, can make him beare the title of a king, and with my body give him possession of a great kingdome, and goodly province. Think then, my Lord, how much I account of your alliance, who being accustomed with the sword to pursue such as durst imbolden themselves to win my love, it is to you only to whom I make a present both of my kisses, imbracings, scepter, and crown: what man is he, if he be not made of stone, that would refuse so precious a pawn as Hermetrude, with the kingdome of Scotland? accept, sweete king, accepte this queene, who with so great love and amitie, desireth your so great profit, and can give you more contentment in one day then the princesse of England wold yeeld you pleasure during her life: although shee surpass me in beauty, her bloud beeing base it is fitter for such a king as you are to chuse Hermetrude, lesse beautiful but noble and famous, rather then the English lady with great beawtie, but issuing from an unknown race, without any title of honor.

Now think if the Dane, hearing such forcible resons and understanding that by her which he half doubted, as also moved with choller for the treason of his father in law, that purposely sent him thether to loose his life, and being welcomed, kist, and playd withal by this queen, yong and reasonable fair, if he were not easie enough to be converted, and like to forget the affection of his first wife, with this to enjoy the realme of Scotland, and so open the waie to become king of all Greate Britain: that, to conclude, he marryed her, and led her with him to the king of Englands court, which moved the king from that time forward much more to seek the meanes to bereave him of his life; and had surely done it, if his daughter, Hamlets other wife, more careful of him that had rejected her then

of her fathers welfare, had not discovered the enterprise
to Hamlet, saying: I know well, my Lord, that the allurements and perswasions of a bold and altogether shameles
woman, being more lascivious then the chast imbrace-
ments of a lawful and modest wife, are of more force to
intice and charm the sences of yong men; but for my part, I
cannot take this abuse for satisfaction, to leave mee in this
sorte without all cause, reason, or precedent faulte once
known in mee, your loyall spouse, and take more pleasure
in the aliance of her who one day will be the cause of your
ruine and overthrow. And although a just cause of jealou-
sye and reasonable motion of anger, dispence with mee at
this time to make no more account of you then you do of
me, that am not worthy to be so scornfully rejected; yet
matrimoniall charitie shal have more force and vigour in
my hart, then the disdaine which I have justly conceived
to see a concubine hold my place, and a strange woman
before my face injoy the pleasures of my husband. This
injury, my Lord, although great and offensive, which to
revenge divers ladies of great renown have in times past
sought and procured the death of their husbands, cannot so much restrain my good wil, but that [I] may not
chuse but advertise you what treason is devised against
you, beseeching you to stand upon your guard, for that my
fathers onely seeking is to bereave you of your life, which
if it happen, I shall not long live after you. Manie reasons
induce me to love and cherish you, and those of great consequence, but especially and above all the rest, I am and
must bee carefull of you, when I feele your child stirring

in my wombe; for which respecte, without so much forgetting yourselfe, you ought to make more account of me
then of your concubine, whome I will love because you
love her, contenting my selfe that your sonne hateth her,
in regard of the wrong she doth to his mother; for it is
impossible that any passion or trouble of the mind whatsoever can quench those fierce passions of love that made
me yours, neither that I shold forget your favours past,
when loyallie you sought the love of the daughter of the
king of England. Neither is it in the power of that thiefe
that hath stoln your heart, nor my fathers choller, to hinder me from seeking to preserve you from the cruelty of
your dissembling friend (as heeretofore by counterfetting
the madman, you prevented the practices and treasons
of your uncle Fengon), the complot being determined to
be executed upon you and yours. Without this advertise-
ment, the Dane had surely been slain, and the Scots that
came with him; for the king of England, inviting his son
in law to a banquet, with greatest curtesies that a friend
can use to him whom he loved as himself, had the means
to intrap him, and cause him dance a pittiful galliard, in
that sort to celebrate the marriage betweene him and his
new lady. But Hamlet went thither with armour under his
clothes, and his men in like sort; by which means he and
his escaped with little hurt, and so after that hapned the
battaile before spoken of, wherein the king of England
losing his life, his countrie was the third time sacked by
the barbarians of the ilands and countrie of Denmark.

Chapter VIII

How Hamblet being in Denmarke, was assailed by Wiglerus his Uncle, and after betrayed by his last wife, called Hermetrude, and was slaine: after whose death she marryed his enemie, Wiglerus.

HAMLET having obtained the victory against the king of England, and slaine him, laden with great treasures and accompanied with his two wives, set forward to saile into Denmarke, but by the way hee had intelligence that Wiglere, his uncle, and sonne to Rodericke, having taken the royall treasure from his sister Geruth (mother to Hamblet) had also seazed upon the kingdome, saying, that neither Horvendile nor any of his helde it but by permission, and that it was in him (to whom the property belonged) to give the charge therof to whom he would. But Hamblet, not desirous to have any quarrell with the sonne of him from whom his predecessors had received their greatnes and advancement, gave such and so rich presents to Wiglere, that he, being contented, withdrew himselfe out of the countrey and territories of Geruths sonne. But within certaine time after, Wiglere, desirous to keepe all the countrey in subjection, intyced by the conquest of Scanie and Sialandie, and also that Hermetrude (the wife of Hamlet, whom he loved more then himselfe) had secret intelligence with him, and had promised him marriage, so that he would take her out of the handes of him that held her, sent to defie Hamlet, and proclaimed open warre against him. Hamlet, like a good and wise prince, loving especially the welfare of his subjects, sought by all meanes to avoyde that warre; but againe refusing it, he perceived a great spot and blemish in his honor, and, accepting the same, he knewe it would bee the ende of his dayes. By the desire of preserving his life on the one side, and his honor on the other side pricking him forward, but, at the last, remembering that never any danger whatsoever had once shaken his vertues and constancy, chose rather the necessitie of his ruine, then to loose the immortal fame that valiant and honourable men obtained in the warres. And there is as much difference betweene a life without honour and an honourable death, as glory and renowne is more excellent then dishonour and evil report.

But the thing that spoyled this vertuous prince was the over great trust and confidence hee had in his wife Hermetrude, and the vehement love hee bare unto her, not once repenting the wrong in that case done to his lawfull spouse, and for the which (paradventure that misfortune had never hapned unto him, and it would never have bin thought that she, whom he loved above all things, would have so villainously betrayed him), hee not once remembring his first wives speeches, who prophesied unto him, that the pleasures hee seemed to take in his other wife would in the end be the cause of his overthrowe, as they had ravished him of the best part of his sences, and quenched in him the great prudence that made him admirable in all the countries in the ocean seas, and through all Germany. Now, the greatest grief that this king (besotted on his wife) had, was the separation of her whom he adored, and, assuring himselfe of his overthrowe, was desirous either that she might beare him company at his death, or els to find her a husband that should love her (he beeing dead) as well as ever hee did. But the disloyall queene had already provided herself of a marriage to put her husband out of trouble and care for that, who perceiving him to be sad for her sake, when shee should have absented her selfe from him, she, to blind him the more and to incourage him to set forward to his owne destruction, promised to follow him whether soever he went, and to take the like fortune that befell to him, were it good or evil, and that so she would give him cause to know how much shee surpassed the English woman in her affection towardes him, saying, that woman is accursed that feareth to follow and accompany her husband to the death: so that, to heare her speake, men would have sayd that shee had been the wife of Mithridates, or Zenobia queene of Palmira, shee made so greate a show of love and constancy. But by the effect it was after easily perceived howe vaine the promise of this unconstant and wavering princesse was; and howe uncomparable the life of this Scottish queene was to the vigor of her chastitie, being a mayd before she was marryed. For that Hamlet had no sooner entred into the field, but she found meanes to see Wiglere, and the battel begun, wherein the miserable Danish prince was slaine; but Hermetrude presently yeelded her self, with all her dead husbands treasons, into the hand of the tyrant, who, more then content with that metamorphosis so much desired, gave order that presently the marriage (bought with the blood and treason of the sonne of Horvendile) should bee celebrated.

Thus you see that there is no promise or determination

of a woman, but that a very small discommoditie of fortune mollifieth and altereth the same, and which time doeth not pervert; so that the misfortunes subject to a constant man shake and overthrowe the naturall slipperie loyaltie of the variable steppes of women, wholy without and any faithfull assurance of love, or true unfained constancy: for as a woman is ready to promise, so is shee heavy and slowe to performe and effect that which she hath promised, as she that is without end or limit in her desires, flattring her selfe in the diversitie of her wanton delights, and taking pleasure in diversitie and change of newe things, which as soone shee doth forget and growe weary off: and, to conclude, such shee is in all her actions, she is rash, covetous, and unthankefull, whatsoever good or service can bee done unto her. But nowe I perceive I erre in my discourse, vomitting such things unworthy of this sects; but the vices of Hermetrude have made mee say more then I meant to speake, as also the authour, from whence I take this Hystorie, hath almost made mee hold this course, I find so great a sweetnesse and livelinesse in this kinde of argument; and the rather because it seemeth so much the truer, considering the miserable successe of poore king Hamlet.

Such was the ende of Hamlet, sonne to Horvendile, prince of Jutie; to whom, if his fortune had been equall with his inward and naturall giftes, I know not which of the auncient Grecians and Romans had been able to have compared with him for vertue and excellencie: but hard fortune following him in all his actions, and yet hee vanquishing the malice of his time with the vigour of constancy, hath left us a notable example of haughtie courage, worthy of a great prince, arming himselfe with hope in things that were wholy without any colour or shewe thereof, and in all his honorable actions made himselfe worthy of perpetuall memorie, if one onely spotte had not blemished and darkened a good part of his prayses. For that the greatest victorie that a man can obtaine is to make himselfe victorious and lord over his owne affections, and that restraineth the unbridled desires of his concupiscence; for if a man be never so princely, valiant, and wise, if the desires and inticements of his flesh prevaile, and have the upper hand, hee will imbase his credite, and, gasing after strange beauties, become a foole, and (as it were) incensed, dote on the presence of women. This fault was in the great Hercules, Sampson; and the wisest man that ever lived upon the earth, following this traine, therein impaired his wit; and the most noble, wise, valiant, and discreet personages of our time, following the same course, have left us many notable examples of their worthy and notable vertues.

But I beseech you that shall reade this Hystorie not to resemble the spider, that feedeth of the corruption that shee findeth in the flowers and fruites that are in the gardens, whereas the bee gathereth her hony out of the best and fayrest flower shee can finde: for a man that is well brought up should reade the lives of whoremongers, drunkards, incestuous, violent, and bloody persons, not to follow their steps, and so to defile himselfe with such uncleannesse, but to shunne paliardize, abstain the superfluities and drunkennesse in banquets, and follow the modestie, courtesie, and continencie that recommendeth Hamlet in this discourse, who, while other made good cheare, continued sober; and where all men sought as much as they could to gather together riches and treasure, hee, simply accounting riches nothing comparable to honor, sought to gather a multitude of vertues, that might make him equall to those that by them were esteemed as gods; having not as then received the lighte of the gospell, that men might see among the barbarians, and them that were farre from the knowledge of one onelye God, that nature was provoked to follow that which is good, and those forward to imbrace vertue, for that there was never any nation, how rude or barbarous soever, that tooke not some pleasure to do that which seemed good, therby to win praise and commendations, which wee have said to be the reward of vertue and good life. I delight to speak of these strange histories, and of people that were unchristned,that the vertue of the rude people maie give more splendor to our nation, who seeing them so compleat, wise, prudent, and well advised in their actions, might strive not only to follow (imitation being a small matter), but to surmount them, as our religion surpasseth their superstition, and our age more purged, subtill, and gallant, then the season wherin they lived and made their vertues knowne.

FINIS.

17231111R00071

Printed in Great Britain
by Amazon